P9-BXZ-353

TED WILLIAMS
with
JIM PRIME

First published in 1995 by
Stoddart Publishing Co. Limited
34 Lesmill Road
Toronto, Canada
M3B 2T6
Tel. (416) 445-3333
Fax (416) 445-5967

Canadian Cataloguing in Publication Data

Williams, Ted, 1918-
Ted Williams' hit list

ISBN 0-7737-5715-5

1. Baseball players - United States - Biography.
I. Prime, Jim. II. Title.

GV865.A1W5 1995   796.357'092'273   C94-932857-X

Cover design: Bill Douglas/The Bang
Typesetting: Brant Cowie/ArtPlus Ltd.
Printed and bound in Canada

Credits: pages 11-12 from *The Mick*, copyright © 1985, by Mickey Mantle with Herb Gluck. Used by permission of Doubleday, a division of Bantam Doubleday Dell Publishing Group, Inc.; page 12 from *Willie Mays: My Life In and Out of Baseball* by Willie Mays as told to Charles Einstein. Copyright © 1966, 1972 by Willie Mays. Used by permission of Dutton Signet, a division of Penguin Books USA Inc.; pages 16-17 from "From .400 to 75, Ted Williams Still Battling Against the Odds" by Dave Anderson, May 22, 1994. Copyright © 1994 by The New York Times Company. Reprinted by permission. Every reasonable effort has been made to obtain reprint permissions. The publisher will gladly receive information that will help rectify any inadvertent errors or omissions in subsequent editions.

To the young baseball players across North America and around the world. I hope these insights into the game's greatest hitters serve to inspire them as they pursue their own baseball dreams.

TED WILLIAMS

For Glenna, Catherine, and Jeffrey, my steadfast supporting lineup. And for my parents, Curtis and Elsie, who showed me that baseball dreams can come true, even those dreamed on the rocky shores of the Bay of Fundy.

JIM PRIME

Contents

+++++++++++++++++++++++++++++++++

Introduction

Ted Williams and Hitting

by Jim Prime

"Aladdin had his wonderful lamp, King Arthur had Excalibur, and Ted Williams had his bat."

— BOSTON SPORTSWRITER HAROLD KAESE

n his opening word to this book, Ted Williams makes an astonishing statement. He says he agreed to write it because he "wanted to contribute something to the lore of baseball." In actual fact, every time he picked up a bat for 19 unforgettable seasons, he did just that.

But Ted was much more than just another sports hero. Like his contemporary, Joe DiMaggio, he symbolizes an exciting, turbulent period in American life. Unlike Joltin' Joe, however, Terrible Ted wasn't always identified with the lofty ideals of sport in the sanitized '40s and '50s. Because his complexity confounded the precise literary labels bestowed on athletic heroes of the day, he was alternately deified and crucified by the Boston media.

Williams seemed driven to excellence by some unspoken and unrelenting force, and with an intensity so singular that it alienated the very profession that should have heralded his brilliance. Cast as a rebel, he was nonetheless more representative of his time, with all its turmoil and social change, than was the Yankee Clipper from New York. DiMaggio symbolized America as Camelot; Williams' America was grittier, less idyllic.

It's hardly surprising that Simon and Garfunkel chose to make lyrical inquiries regarding the whereabouts of Joe DiMaggio rather than Ted Williams. The Williams persona doesn't fit snugly into carefree rhyme the way DiMaggio's did. Perhaps an epic poem could do him justice — or a grand opera.

There was never anything phony about Ted. He was always brutally honest with the press and with fans. Unfortunately his candor was often portrayed as arrogance, especially in the competitive New England newspaper market where his every utterance became front page news. The result was a love-hate relationship with the Fenway Faithful.

In a classic piece of 1960 sports reporting, Pulitzer prizewinning novelist John Updike described Ted Williams' last game as a member of the Boston Red Sox. What could have been just another maudlin farewell to past glory became much more when Williams' on-field heroics were transmitted through Updike's talented pen.

In the young writer's eyes this single tumultuous game became an eloquent metaphor for a tumultuous career. Weaving rare insights into his nine-inning narrative, he created a revealing portrait of baseball's most complex personality.

Updike underscored Williams' stormy relationship with both press and fans and conveyed the impact he had made on the game. He then described the drama of Williams' last fateful major league swing and captured in a single phrase the rationale for Ted's stubborn refusal to tip his hat to the adoring fans after the resultant home run. "Gods do not answer letters," was Updike's concise conclusion.

Up until 1981 I took Updike's ecclesiastical explanation quite literally. From what I had read and heard about my hero, Ted Williams wasn't one to dash off spontaneous notes to a Nova Scotia fan. Twenty baseball seasons had then entered the record books since the erstwhile Kid last swung a bat in anger for the Boston Red Sox. I had followed Ted's retirement through the pages of *Sports Illustrated* and knew that he divided his time between the Florida Keys and the Miramichi River in the Canadian province of New Brunswick. He didn't so much travel as migrate, a willing slave to the aquatic habits of bonefish, tarpon and Atlantic salmon. It was the latter species which brought him within striking distance of me. The Miramichi River is generally acknowledged to be the finest Atlantic-salmon stream in the world. It draws sportsmen from across the continent to its shores, and foremost among them is Williams, who returns to the river each year with the tenacity and persistence of the fish which made it famous.

Despite my lack of faith in a reply, I wrote Ted a combination fan letter and interview request, taking elaborate pains to disassociate myself from those pushy Boston media types who, I commiserated, had made his life as a player a living hell. I then promptly forgot the whole thing, such was my level of confidence in any answer.

And then it arrived, a succinct, handwritten letter from a baseball god. Divine intervention in a plain white envelope:

Dear Jim,

Got your letter and will be happy to talk to you. Phone or otherwise.
I'm not as mean and ornery as you might think.

— Ted Williams

In spite of his written assurance, it was with some degree of anxiety that I awaited my initial meeting with one of baseball's immortals. After all, the very mention of his name evokes a flood of images for an entire generation of North Americans: the Splendid Splinter, The Kid, The Thumper, Teddy Ballgame, The Big Guy, Terrible Ted. It was that last appellation which caused me some concern. For a writer, the name Ted Williams holds special significance. Those well-documented battles with the Boston press gave me pause to consider a quick retreat. After all, his hatred of writers had been profound and apparently indiscriminate.

My fears were gradually allayed as Ted welcomed me to his fishing lodge and introduced me to his longtime guide Roy Curtis. "Jim," he sniffed in exaggerated contempt, "is a writer." Although the sobriquet "Splinter" may no longer apply, Ted Williams remains a splendid and imposing figure. At 6'4", with healthy, tanned face, thick black hair speckled with white, and a booming John Wayne voice, he is truly larger than life. He fills a room with his presence.

Soon we were on the way to Ted's favorite salmon pool, and the subject turned to his first love, *Salmo salar* — the Atlantic salmon. He pursues the fish with a passion born of respect and fascination. "It's a romantic sort of fish, you know," says Williams. "It sets its mind on a goal and nothing gets in the way of that goal. It doesn't discourage easily."

Neither does Williams. In 1958, after capturing the American League batting title on the last day of the season in Washington, D.C., he caught a flight to Boston, changed planes for the trip to Bangor, Maine, and finally arrived on the Miramichi at 2:30 the next afternoon, only two hours before the salmon season was to close. His single-minded tenacity was rewarded with a prize 20-lb hookbill. Little wonder that Williams is as much a part of this storied river as the fish which first drew him there.

Since our initial meeting I have enjoyed several memorable trips to Ted's fishing lodge in Blackville, N.B. He and his friend Louise Kaufman were always gracious hosts, and the visitors to his home have been a diverse and stimulating cross section of North American society. Doctors and lawyers mingle with slaughterhouse owners, salesmen, and fishing guides — all with two things in common, a love of salmon fishing and a feeling of kinship with Ted Williams.

The idea for this book was spawned after my second pilgrimage to the Miramichi. In the course of our conversations, it was becoming obvious that Ted's knowledge of hitters was not confined to his own league or even his own era. He enjoyed talking about the feats of Musial, Mantle, DiMaggio, and Cobb every bit as much as he enjoyed recalling his own career. He was continually making comparisons, rating hitters in various categories, analyzing techniques, questioning the "baseballic" intelligence of various batters.

The idea hit me with the force of a Sandy Koufax fastball: Why not record these insights from a baseball god? The result was *Ted Williams' Hit List*. It may not possess quite the historical significance of the Ten Commandments, but in baseball circles it will carry just about as much authority. After all, Moses may have had sin pretty well covered but he knew almost nothing about the impact of the slider.

Ted agreed to tackle the project, I believe, because he genuinely loves to talk about hitting and does so with the fervor of a religious zealot. He had told his own life story in *My Turn at Bat* and had examined the process of hitting in *The Science of Hitting*. The only thing left was to turn his expertise to a rating of the great hitters.

Ted's credentials for such a project are unmatched. Other books on the great hitters have been compiled by writers, those "Knights of the Keyboard" whose baseball savvy Ted has thrown into disrepute more than once over the years. Williams qualifies as the ultimate authority on hitting. He is to hitting what Pavarotti is to opera and what Johnny Carson was to late-night TV. He knows more about the art and science of bat meeting ball than any other man alive. Throughout his career he was constantly sought out by teammates and opposing players for advice on how to cure a slump. He could detect even the most subtle of flaws in a player's swing and, like some baseball version of a faith healer, send him forth with new insights and newfound confidence — a born-again hitter.

Carl Yastrzemski, in his book *Yaz: Baseball, The Wall, and Me*, provides a telling account of one such miracle cure while he was mired in a devastating slump during his rookie career with the Red Sox. Hitting an anemic .220, he was seriously starting to question his ability to play in the major leagues. Immediately the call went out from owner Tom Yawkey to Ted Williams, whom Yaz had replaced as the Bosox left fielder. After a three-day search Ted was located on a Florida fishing trip and flown to Boston. The slump doctor was making a house call. Dispensing his usual hitting prescriptions and a large dose of confidence, he watched his patient make an amazing recovery. Yaz went on a July hitting rampage, batting at a sizzling .478 clip with 22 hits in 46 at-bats and watching his average rise from .236 to a respectable .269.

As if that weren't proof enough of Ted's knowledge of hitting and hitters, the remarkable case of the '69 Washington Senators leaves no room for further doubt. With Williams as manager and hitting coach, the lowly Senators went from a combined batting average of .224 to a respectable .251 in a single year, the baseball equivalent of rags to riches. Significantly, every single member of that team showed improved hitting statistics over the previous campaign: Eddie Brinkman went from .187 to .266, Frank Howard from .274 to .298, Mike Epstein from .234 to .278, Del Unser from .230 to .286, Hank Allen from .219 to .278, and Ken McMullen from .248 to .272.

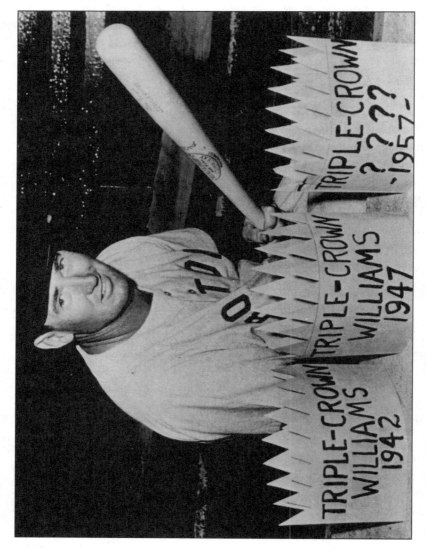

Despite falling short in '57, Ted was hitting royalty. BETTMANN ARCHIVE

It is probable that Ted has influenced the careers of more young hitters than all other hitting theorists combined. His disciples are legion, and his book *The Science of Hitting* is still — despite a growing number of heretical alternatives — the Bible of batting. Even today, 35 years after his retirement, no serious discussion of hitting can take place without evoking Williams' theories. Ted practiced at the plate what he now preaches, and his record stands as testament to the effectiveness of his approach. During his 19-year assault on American League pitchers, he hit 521 home runs, maintained a .344 average, and remains the last man in the majors to hit .400 over an entire season. He was American League batting champ six times, home run champ four times, American League MVP in '46 and '49, and was chosen to the American League All-Star squad 16 times. His career was punctuated by dramatic hits — usually home runs — and the final homer, in his last major league at-bat, provided a fitting exclamation mark to an amazing hitting odyssey. In 1966 he was elected to the Hall of Fame. His ponderous record becomes all the more remarkable when you realize that fully five years were cut from the heart of his career through service in the Second World War and Korea.

Ted's oft-quoted goal was to walk down the street and have people acknowledge him as the greatest hitter the game has ever known. Today, on every thoroughfare from Pennsylvania Avenue to Wall Street to Route 66 to Sesame Street, it would be easy to find people only too happy to tip a respectful hat to Williams. People like Mickey Mantle, Joe DiMaggio, Carl Yastrzemski, Bob Feller, and former president George Bush, to name just a few.

But what about Ted? Does *he* think he reached that brash goal he set for himself so long ago? Did he include himself on his Hit List? Certainly it would be hard for any knowledgeable baseball fan to imagine a book on the great hitters that does not include Ted Williams, but he strongly resisted any suggestion that he should insert himself in the rankings. When I asked Ted point-blank if he felt that he had achieved that long-ago ambition, he considered the question for a long moment before answering.

Well, you know, in my heart I don't know if I did or not. In my heart I really don't. I do know that I was

one of the best hitters that ever played this game. If I was as good a hitter as Gehrig, or as good a hitter as Cobb or Foxx, I would indeed feel that I was in select company.

I will say this much: There's no question that the two premier hitters for 15 years in the American League were DiMaggio and Williams.

I had natural talent, I don't think there's any question about that, but I want to tell you something: A lot of guys had as much goddamn talent as I had, I'm convinced of that. It takes more than natural ability to excel as a hitter.

This is all I can say about me: I know I could hit a fastball with anybody who ever played. I know that, even though I hit off the slider the last 12 years of my career. I think I was an intelligent hitter. But probably as important as anything else is the fact that nobody ever lived who had more opportunity to swing the bat than Ted Williams. And that's what I could do. It's the *only* goddamn thing that I could do well, and it's the only thing that I really *wanted* to do. I was lucky enough to earn a good living doing what I was born to do.

I had an inquisitive — and I don't want to say studious — mind, but the only real subject that triggered me to find out as much as I could about it, and the only thing that really motivated me to be as good as I could at it, was hitting a baseball. Now that's all I can say, or want to say, about me.

Fortunately Ted's contemporaries were much less reticent about Ted's hitting prowess and his place among the all-time greats. Among the Hall of Famers who have gone to bat for Williams are Hank Aaron, Stan Musial, Mickey Mantle, Joe DiMaggio, Bob Feller, Tris Speaker, and Willie Mays.

I asked Aaron for his thoughts, and the Home Run King left little doubt where he stood on the matter:

Ted was probably the greatest hitter I have ever seen. In fact you'd have to say that he was probably the number one hitter of all time. I was impressed every time I saw Ted. He was an amazing hitter. He had the quickest bat I ever saw. That's one reason why they put the shift on him. With Ted it didn't matter if the pitcher was left-handed or right-handed.

I liked a lot of things about Ted but the one thing that he and I had in common was the fact that I kind of isolated myself away from pitchers, I just didn't feel that I should be friendly with them. And I think Ted felt the same way. We both felt that they were our worst enemy, that they'd go back and tell each other how to get you out.

Stan Musial, his chief National League rival, was equally effusive in his praise for Williams the hitter:

Ted was a once-in-a-generation hitter, the best of our time, without question. He knew his art and knew his pitchers. He had a keen appreciation of the strike zone, a great eye, quick hands — and what power! It's no accident that he hit .400. If he hadn't missed almost five years because of military service in World War II and Korea he might have hit 700 home runs. Even so, he is tied for tenth place on the all-time list with 521 and a career average of .344, the sixth highest. I've always thought there were three reasons for his success: He had the most ability, he worked harder than anyone else, and he said his ambition was to be able to walk down the street after his career and hear people say, "There goes the greatest hitter who ever lived." In my opinion, he reached that goal.

In his book, *The Mick,* Mickey Mantle called Ted

an Einstein at the bat. Precise, mechanically perfect, every swing beautifully executed. I still marvel at the way he used to stand up there, leaning in, shoulders held high, the bat cocked, ready to whip around as though guided by a computer. Swish! You had to see him to know he was the very best and I doubt if there will be another one like him on the scene for a long, long while.

He went on to say, "He's my number one idol, the greatest hitter that ever lived — or at least the greatest that I saw."

In *Willie Mays: My Life In and Out of Baseball* (by Willie Mays as told to Charles Einstein), Mays describes the first major league game he ever saw:

I went out to watch the Browns play the Red Sox. I got there early, and it had to be the 10 or 15 most wonderful moments of my life, watching Ted Williams in batting practice. This has got to be the most perfect batting swing in all baseball history. I just sat there with my mouth open. The wrist action was all the more amazing because, like most great hitters, you couldn't even see his wrists. His arms, the forearms, seemed like they just came down in two straight columns of muscle to his hands.

Ted's greatest antagonist, Joe DiMaggio, has called him "the best hitter I ever saw. There was nobody like him."

Representing the pitching fraternity that had to face him, Bob Feller says "he was the best hitter that I ever pitched to. . . . There wasn't a pitch he couldn't hit. He had no weaknesses."

Even old-timers like Ty Cobb and Tris Speaker sang his praises. Cobb once observed, "Ted is one of the greatest natural hitters I've ever seen. If he'd hit to left field, he'd break up that (Boudreau) shift and break every record in the book. He'd hit .500."

Speaker said that he "had seen them all" and suggested that Ted

was in a class by himself. If he'd had the opportunity to play right through his career like Ruth and most of the other great hitters did, his records would be all the more amazing. He had to make the grade five times: when he came up, when he returned from

World War II, after he broke his elbow, when he returned from Korea, and after breaking his shoulder. Amazing. Williams was just out of this world as a hitter, the best of them all. (Source: *The Picture History of the Boston Red Sox,* by George Sullivan)

No two baseball minds could be more opposite than arch-conservative Ted Williams and ultimate liberal Bill Lee. Lee, the erstwhile Spaceman who toiled for the Red Sox and Montreal Expos in the '70s and '80s, was well known for his defiance of authority and for his bohemian lifestyle. He once admitted to sprinkling hashish on his organic buckwheat pancakes so that he would be impervious to the bus fumes when he ran to the ballpark.

In 1988 the southpaw was running for the presidency of the United States on the highly farcical Rhinoceros Party of Canada ticket. I asked him what his platform would be. "No guns, no butter — they'll both kill you. Tear down defenses. Ted Williams will be my Secretary of Defense. He'll go out and tear down all defenses like he did when he was playing baseball." This cryptic reference to Ted's dismantling of Lou Boudreau's infamous "Williams Shift," coming from such a decidedly left-wing source, is eloquent testimony to the way in which hero worship can bridge even the widest political schism.

Perhaps it's fitting to have Carl Yastrzemski, the man who had the daunting task of filling Williams' shoes in Boston, have the last word. In his autobiography, *Yaz,* he says,

They can talk about Babe Ruth and Ty Cobb and Rogers Hornsby and Lou Gehrig and Joe DiMaggio and Stan Musial and all the rest, but I'm sure not one of them could hold cards and spades to Williams in his sheer knowledge of the hitting, of how to read pitchers, of what to expect and why to expect it, of how to cover every fraction of an inch of the strike zone, of when to swing for homers and when to settle for something else, of how to pull out of slumps, and of every other conceivable facet of the art of hitting a baseball. He studied hitting the way a broker studies

the stock market, and could spot at a glance the mistakes that others couldn't see in a week.

Who better to compile a list of the greatest hitters than one of their number, one whose quest to be the best led him to learn at the feet of giants such as Cobb, Hornsby, Terry, and Collins. Someone who played with and against some of the best hitters of any era: Musial, DiMaggio, Foxx, Mantle, and other Hall of Fame sluggers. Someone respected by his peers as the best hitter of them all. Someone whose interest in the subject of hitting remains as keen as his batting eye once was. For Ted Williams, hitting was always the number one consideration, the engine that drove the game of baseball.

Get Ted talking about hitting and he becomes as focused as anyone can ever get on any subject. When he analyzes hitters he does so with a frankness and objectivity that leaves no room for sentiment. Yet he can become as animated and nostalgic at the recalled image of a Foxx or Mantle homer as for any of the 521 that he hit himself.

Ted Williams was not only a logical choice to undertake this project, he was the ideal choice — the only real choice. He is a person who examines everything, questions everything, studies everything, and does it all with complete candor and no hidden agendas.

Typical of this candor was Ted's response when I once pushed him to compare his career with that of fellow Hall of Famer Carl Yastrzemski, the man who replaced him in Fenway Park's left field. Instead of spouting the usual platitudes, Ted gave me his frank, brutally honest assessment, totally without animosity and supported by irrefutable fact.

> **I think we should understand each other, you and I, well enough to know that I may make a statement that doesn't sound altogether complimentary to somebody but it's a fact. *You* mentioned it! Hell, Yaz got a home run every 26 or 27 times at the plate. He's been up over 4000 more times than I have and has driven in only five more runs [Yaz drove in 1844**

Ted Williams practices what he preaches. AP/WIDE WORLD PHOTOS compared to Williams' 1839], hasn't hit as many home runs [Yaz stroked 452 and Ted 521], and with his .285 average he's hit sixty points less lifetime average than I did. I would be the very first to admit that Yaz was a great all-round player, but all you have to do is look at his offensive statistics. That's why I say you have to be fair about the way you're comparing these guys.

That's when I knew Ted could offer something refreshingly new: honesty. No false modesty. No polite clichés. Certainly no political correctness. Just Ted Williams telling it like it is. He doesn't need to do more and is incapable of doing less. After all, as I found out first-hand, his place in baseball history is secure.

Following my initial meeting with Ted several years ago, his name became familiar around our household. I discovered just how familiar when we journeyed to Boston's Fenway Park in 1983 to see the Red Sox play Kansas City. By the third inning our three-year-old daughter had dozed off in the August sun, just as Carl Yastrzemski hit a long home run into the right-field bleachers. Abruptly awakened by the capacity crowd's deafening salute to another Red Sox legend in the final year of his career, she joined in the spirit of celebration with words that almost certainly hadn't been spoken at revered old Fenway since the Splendid Splinter homered in his last at-bat on September 26, 1960. "Hooray for Ted Williams," said Catherine Jane Prime. "Hooray for Ted Williams."

Postscript: In February of 1994, Ted, then 75 years old, suffered a serious stroke that landed him in the hospital, "in a bed that's too short," hooked up to an assortment of tubes and wires. In a *New York Times* article Ted related the following revealing story to writer Dave Anderson. It may be the ultimate proof that Williams and hitting can't be separated:

I'm half asleep. I dream I'm in spring training working with the young Red Sox hitters like I did for years. But somehow Randy Johnson is out there on the mound, the big left-hander with Seattle that the guy on the Phillies bailed out on in the All-Star Game last year. John Kruk wanted no part of that big left-hander.

Now with Johnson out there, all the Red Sox kids are saying, "Why don't you go up there and take a few cuts?"

I tell them, "I haven't hit in years and I just had a stroke and I can't see too well," but they keep teasing me and I say, "Yeah, I'll do it." But as I'm walking to home plate, I'm thinking, "I'm not going to try to pull this guy because he can really throw." The first pitch, he laid one right in there. I pushed at it. Line drive through the box for a base hit.

An Opening Word

by Ted Williams

The prime interest of my life is baseball, and to me the heart of baseball is hitting. That is what this book is all about. With all due respect to my good friends in the pitching brotherhood, the way you excel most prominently and most effectively as a big league ballplayer is by being able to hit. That is what fans come to the major league ballparks to see. The *hitters* are the ones people talk about, and in all the great franchises the hitters made the town.

Mays and Aaron and DiMaggio rank high as all-round players. They could do it all on the basepaths and in the field — but don't forget one thing: All those guys were great hitters, and if they couldn't have hit nobody would have ever heard of them.

Most of the books on the great hitters have been produced by writers. Some are very good and some aren't quite so good, but *Ted Williams' Hit List* is different because it is written from a hitter's point of view.

I agreed to write this book with Jim Prime because I wanted to contribute something to the lore of baseball. In Jim I met a guy who I knew was very, very interested in the whole subject of hitters and hitting. A knowledgeable guy who loves the game of baseball. He put some new ideas in my face and he's the most persistent son of a bitch I ever met in my life. I wasn't able to get rid of him and for a while it looked like this book wouldn't be completed before the year 2000 because of his persistence.

But there is another reason why I agreed to author this book. I truly feel that the technique of hitting has — in my eyes — deteriorated over the last 35 or 40 years. I see that gradual decline and it concerns me. I see hitters not taking advantage of the pitch; hitters not hitting according to the type of pitcher they're hitting against; hitters not compensating for different styles of pitching, different kinds of deliveries. I see hitters not hitting according to the count; hitters not hitting according to the wind and other conditions; hitters not hitting according to the dimensions of the ballpark. Hitters apparently not even realizing what they did the last time at bat! And on and on.

When they fail to recognize these and other factors, they miss out on some definite advantages which could help them get an edge on the pitcher their next time at bat. If a pitcher gets you out on two half-assed curves in a row, you should be prepared to lay back for that pitch at least for one strike. Or maybe two strikes if you still had confidence that you could hit this guy with two strikes. If it's 592' to right field and 375' to left field, I'm not going to try to pull the hell out of the ball to right. I might as well hit a little more straight away, especially if the wind favors me in that direction.

It's all part of a learning process for hitters. There's a period where you don't jump on your mistakes as quickly as you should. The first three years would be a real learning cycle — just trying to get it going. Then, somewhere along the line, things start to gel for a hitter. Naturally there will be ups and downs, injuries that will set you back or other things that keep you out of the lineup. Those are things you have to learn to cope with as you go along. But I've seen too many hitters waste too many years learning simple, easy things and making the same mistakes for six years longer than they should have, and not really getting the end results they were physically capable of achieving.

It's that type of thing — proper thinking — that is lacking in today's hitters. I see good swings, I see great speed, I see great talent. I see an awful lot of things that would just make me rub my hands in glee and delight, and I think, "Boy, look at *this* guy!" And then invariably he fails. This is one of the saddest things for me in baseball because I see a ton of talent there. Players are bigger, stronger, and faster, but they don't know that little game between the hitter and pitcher.

That's why I'm happy to write about some of the guys I did see play, guys that I saw do what they could do, who strived to make the best use of their God-given talents, to reach their true potential. I feel fortunate to have seen most of the 20 great hitters in this book firsthand, either in batting practice or in actual game situations when I played against them.

And certainly I would have loved to have seen Ruth and Speaker and Hornsby and Cobb and the great Shoeless Joe Jackson in their prime. I'd love to have seen those guys hit. They were the masters, the pioneers who established such high standards for the rest of us.

Having said all that, I never saw a hitter in my life, myself included, who I thought got the one hundred percent best performance out of his capabilities — and I probably never will.

What Makes a Great Hitter?

I said it 30 years ago and I steadfastly believe it today. In fact I've said it so often it could probably serve as my epitaph: Hitting a baseball is the single most difficult thing to do in sport.

My golfing friend Sam Snead once tried to make a case for the unique skills needed to succeed in his genteel sport, but his challenge didn't really impress me. I pointed out that golfers are permitted to hit a stationary ball with a flat-surfaced club, while playing to galleries which remain silent during each swing and then applaud politely regardless of the result.

A hitter, on the other hand, is expected to hit a round ball with a round bat and adjust his swing in a split second to 100-mile-per-hour fastballs, backbreaking curveballs, and, occasionally, knuckleballs that mimic the flight patterns of nearsighted moths. All this, while 50,000 fans are questioning his ancestry and screaming for him to fail. Snead made a last brave attempt to defend the honor of his game — and don't get me wrong, golf *is* a great game — by suggesting that at least I never had to wade into the crowd to play my foul balls. Well, he wasn't going to convert me with *that* stuff. You'd have a better chance of convincing Norman Schwarzkopf that the Bolshoi Ballet is a tougher outfit than the U.S. Marines.

I don't think you have to have been a major league ballplayer to concede my point. Anyone who grew up facing the wild offerings of some rawboned hurler, whether it was in an uneven cow pasture in the Midwest or on a vacant lot in Brooklyn or San Diego, knows exactly what I'm talking about. And anyone who has been humiliated in the batting cage at the county fair, in front of his family or his girlfriend, knows the clear truth of my argument.

Even the vaunted major leaguer who hits at the magic .300 level — and as a result now earns a salary that resembles the gross national product of a small country — fails seven times in every ten at bats. That sort of production would not be tolerated in bowlers, quarterbacks, basketball players, or stockbrokers, and certainly not in golfers. But in baseball these athletes are dubbed superstars and their rookie baseball cards become investment-portfolio starter kits.

In hitting, a .700 futility percentage is a much coveted goal. That tells you something! The fans are willing to accept and appreciate such apparent mediocrity because they know the degree of difficulty involved in hitting a baseball. That's why they applaud such seemingly small mileposts. They know in their hearts that the difference between a .280 hitter and a .300 hitter is more than .020. It's the difference between Bucky Dent and Carl Yastrzemski. Hell, it's the difference between Dom and Joe DiMaggio.

It's obvious to me that those players who excel at such a demanding skill are deserving of special recognition, and that's what this book is all about. But first I'll tell you what this book is *not.* It is not a book which attempts to analyze the greatest all-round players of all time, although many of those included certainly qualify on that count too. There are no "good field, no hit" shortstops or "defensive specialists" included here! Obviously there are no pitchers here either — with the spectacular exception of Babe Ruth, who probably could have made it to Cooperstown as a hurler or a hitter. Greats of the game such as Brooks Robinson, Joe Morgan, and Johnny Bench will not be found between these covers, despite their considerable hitting skills and Hall of Fame credentials in other phases of the game. It's not that those other facets of the game aren't important, but I was a hitter and that's what I know something about.

In fact a lot of truly fine hitters did not find their way onto my Hit List. Pete Rose is conspicuous by his absence. Roberto

Clemente, a fine ballplayer and a finer human being, didn't make the cut. Neither did Ernie Banks, Al Kaline, Rod Carew, Hack Wilson, Paul Molitor, and a veritable galaxy of other bona fide hitting stars. I don't apologize for their absence. It's no oversight — and it's sure no disgrace. It only serves to underscore just how great my top 20 hitters really were.

This is a book about baseball's *greatest* hitters, a tribute from a fellow hitter to that special breed of athlete who has hit the ball harder, farther, and with greater frequency than anyone else in the history of the game. These are the best of the best, the aristocracy of hitting.

Now what made them the best? Over the years much has been made of my three golden rules of hitting: 1) get a good ball to hit; 2) proper thinking at the plate; 3) be quick with the bat. To me those remain the real secrets of hitting. But they don't really tell you what personal characteristics are common to all superior hitters. In my experience all great hitters share certain strengths. I call them my five ingredients, and they practically define a great hitter.

THE FIVE INGREDIENTS

I've always had strong feelings about the attributes needed to become a great hitter. In 1950 *Time* magazine interviewed me for a cover story and asked me to divulge the "secrets of my success" at the plate. At that time I singled out four "ingredients" that I felt made me a successful hitter: courage, eyesight, power, and timing. Today I'd like to confirm those choices and add one more.

Intelligence

Those others are great ingredients, and they are all things that you have to have, but I was very young when I said all of that and there was one glaring omission in my analysis. Today I'd add one more very important component to the mix. The one ingredient that isn't there — the one that separates the really good from the great — is intelligence. And I'm not necessarily talking about rocket science here. I'm talking about baseballic intelligence.

The first four attributes certainly describe what you have to have, but they don't give you the whole meat. You can have those things in spades, but damn it, you've got to know what you're doing at the plate. You've got to be smart. Hitting is 50 percent from the neck up, and knowing what's going on is 50 percent of the battle.

It's a little game, knowing the pitchers, knowing their strengths and their weaknesses, studying their deliveries, and learning how you have to hit certain types of pitchers. Is there such a thing as a dumb good hitter? Well, I've seen guys who could swing the bat and were pretty good natural hitters, and you wonder why they're not even better, why they don't improve. Invariably it's because they're so damn dumb about what's going on. Before long the pitching fraternity catches on and it's all over. They start to go downhill instead of learning and improving. There are dozens of examples to draw from, guys like George Bell. He started out like gangbusters but didn't progress. After a while he just left me cold. I wouldn't have had him on my ballclub.

You see a lot of deficiencies in today's hitters. Some problems are just matters of style — or lack of style. In that regard the biggest fault is not getting their hips ahead of their hands. It should be pretty basic, hips ahead of hands, but I don't always see quite the action there that I'd like. And the number of hitters swinging at too many bad balls has reached epidemic proportions. It makes me cringe to watch some of these guys. The thing is, those are things that can be corrected if you have a hitter who wants to learn and improve.

It's really a symptom of a much bigger malady. The fundamental problem is that hitters quite obviously don't know proper thinking at the plate. By that I mean, for instance, they get the count in their favor against a pitcher and *still* look like they've got two strikes on them. Hell, they may have a pitcher two and nothing and then let him off the hook by swinging at bad pitches. You know the script: Fooled on a pitch! Late on a fastball! Fooled on another pitch! Lunging at pitches that are outside and taking fastballs down the middle for strikes. For *no* reason. In most cases they didn't even know what the situation was, let alone what the pitcher might be throwing in that situation. This isn't some radical new idea. These are basic, elementary, 150-year-old rules we're talking about here.

So baseballic intelligence is a common thread that runs through all great hitters. For some it's almost instinctive, for others it comes about through hard work and a willingness to learn.

Courage

Courage you have to have, that little extra determination, especially when the going is tough and you don't see the pitcher quite as well as you should. Some pitchers have a tight-assed delivery and you don't follow those guys as well.

I was never really afraid at the plate. Good hitters can't afford to be. When you're young you have the really great reflexes and you're confident that you can get out of the road in time. Naturally if you faced a genuinely wild son of a gun, someone that you *knew* was wild, you might be a little more concerned. That's different from a good pitcher who just wants to brush you back and keep you honest. With those guys you might not worry too much; at least I know I wouldn't. But if a guy is just plain wild and you don't know where the hell he's going to throw it, you might be a little looser up there. Especially if he could really throw smoke.

I was beaned once, and all I kept thinking was, "This ain't gonna stop me! This ain't gonna stop me! *This is not going to stop me!*" I kept saying it and saying it. I wasn't going to let anything stop me from being the hitter I hoped to be. That's exactly the way I felt. In fact I remember right after the beaning incident in Milwaukee, we went directly to Kansas City and I played an afternoon game against a left-handed pitcher, and I hung right in there repeating that same phrase over and over: Nothing's going to stop me. And that's what happened. Nothing stopped me! Looking back 40 years later, you have to say that it was a great attitude to have. I never really thought about it at that time, but it was pretty near storybook devotion to the goal I had set for myself. To become the best hitter I could be.

That kind of determination is common to all my top 20 hitters. Aaron had it. Gehrig sure as hell had it, and so did Robinson and the rest. They all overcame obstacles and persevered and eventually came out on top. All my great hitters have to have had courage.

Eyesight

Certainly good eyesight is necessary for a hitter. You need it in order to be able to pick up various pitches and see the spin on the ball. The writers were always quick to credit my eyesight for my hitting, and a lot of rubbish was written about just how good my eyes were. They made it sound as if I had Superman's vision. My eyesight was good, but not *that* good. I hurt my eye when I was a young kid, and there were plenty of times when I couldn't see well that day and still I'd get three hits. It takes a hell of a lot more than good eyesight to hit .400 in the major leagues. But it would be impossible to become a great hitter without it.

Hornsby had exceptional eyesight. So did Mel Ott. I bet if you could have tested the eyes of all of baseball's first-rate hitters, they would all show above-average eyesight.

Power

In that same *Time* magazine story, I talk about power being in the "wrist and forearm." My power was actually generated from hip action. I'm not a muscular guy anyway, and neither was Hank Greenberg or some others on the list. The hips force you to go through the power zone with *power.* If you don't use your hips, you don't have that power. You just pull the bat through. I was certainly very aware of my strength, but more than anything else I wanted to be quick with the bat through the power zone.

The National Leaguers used to tell me what a great hitter Paul Waner was at 155 lbs soaking wet. Waner was a .340 hitter, and even though he didn't have that many home runs, he was so good that I'm not sure he doesn't deserve to be within a line drive of the top 20. For a couple of years he hit 15 or 18 home runs, and Dizzy Dean told me, "Without a doubt, Waner is the greatest hitter I ever pitched to." Now that's quite a statement coming from a Hall of Famer and one of the greatest National League pitchers who ever played. Dean could mow *anybody* down, but regardless of his lack of size, Waner wore him out with his quickness. So bat speed produces power, even in guys who aren't so muscular. You don't have to be built like Paul Bunyan — or even Jose Canseco — to hit home runs, and long ones too.

Timing

As in many things in life, timing is everything for a hitter. Timing comes through practice, practice, practice, and through analyzing what you're doing. Hitting a baseball is difficult because there are so many variables involved, and that's why it requires so much practice in order to improve. I played every month and every day of the year in San Diego. None of the hitters on my list got there without hours and days and years of hard work. You need to take advantage of every opportunity to hone your hitting skills. You need to hit a lot of baseballs and have a lot of baseballs thrown to you. Eventually your sense of timing becomes sharp. It always amazes me — and this is as much a case for a hitter's intelligence as it is for timing — if you ask a lot of today's hitters, "When you hit the ball on the ground, are you generally late or early?" Well some of them are *still* trying to figure it out. There's no question about it: when you hit ground balls, you're much more apt than not to be early. Then you ask them, "When you hit the ball to the opposite field, do you tend to hit it in the air or on the ground?" Well, in the air of course! So if you're a little late on the swing, the tendency is to get it in the air; when you're a little early, the tendency is to hit it on the ground toward some Golden Glove infielder. Just knowing that basic fact puts you ahead of the game. Mel Ott, another little guy, hit over 500 home runs, and he gave most of the credit to timing.

RESULTS ARE WHAT COUNT

If this were a recipe book, I guess you'd just mix those five ingredients together, put them in the oven at 350 degrees, and cook up a great hitter. Well obviously it doesn't work that way. While many players may possess some — or even all — of the qualities that I just identified, only a very select few make full use of them throughout their careers. A bad chef might have the best ingredients in the world, but the results can still prove disastrous.

After all, baseball is not a neat cause-and-effect kind of game. You can't apply a formula — great eyesight + great power + intelligence + courage + timing = a great hitter — to baseball. It's not an exact science. There are still things like heart and desire and dedication and hard work that enter into the equation too. Sometimes a player with only mediocre natural talent can outperform a guy with a ton of God-given ability. I've seen it many times.

That's why the proof of the hitter is in the numbers. Statistics and career records provide concrete, irrefutable evidence of those who were best able to take full advantage of their ability over the long haul. And while it's perfectly true that statistics can't measure intangibles like heart or desire, they can provide you with a yardstick to compare the *results* of a hitter's skill and effort. Nevertheless, I'd be the first to admit that statistics don't tell the whole story. I'll talk more later about the statistical process that was used to help compile the Hit List and establish the rankings.

The Rankings

'Ve come to the conclusion that if hitting a baseball is the most difficult thing to do in sport, then getting two people to agree on who did it best must be a close second. Even if it is possible to identify the top 20 hitters of all time more or less accurately, you'd almost think you were defying the baseball deities the way people react when you try to put them in some actual ranking. Fans take these things seriously, and I *know* how many pitfalls there are in an undertaking like this.

After all, how much drop-off is there from a Cadillac to the very best Buick? There's a little drop-off, but they're still the same basic luxury car. *These* are good, but *those* are the best, that's what it comes down to. And that's what I've done to create the Hit List. After thorough study and careful scrutiny, I've come up with a list of the players that I am convinced are the 20 greatest hitters of all time.

From the first time I swung a bat back in San Diego, throughout my minor and major league career, and during my time as a manager and batting instructor, I've tried to learn all I could about hitters and hitting. I never passed up an opportunity to talk with my contemporaries from both leagues, or with those great old-timers whose eyes lit up when they recalled a Cobb slide or a long homer by the Babe. Even today, if a bright young prospect is genuinely interested and wants to bend my ear on my favorite subject, I won't say no.

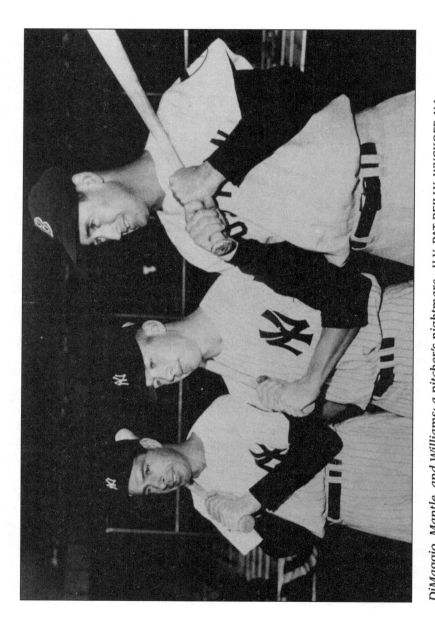

DiMaggio, Mantle, and Williams: a pitcher's nightmare. H.V. PAT REILLY, WYCKOFF, N.J.

I've questioned, I've probed, I've challenged, I've argued, and in my early years I probably made a genuine nuisance of myself with my persistence. But the most important thing I did was listen. And I was a pretty good listener, too. I knew I had a lot to learn, and I couldn't learn it fast enough for my liking. Those conversations were usually focused on the techniques of hitting, but invariably at some point the discussion would come around to specific hitters — what they did and how they did it.

I talked at length with Cobb and with Hornsby and Collins and a host of other early legends of the game, and I drew heavily on those memorable conversations when the time came to evaluate the dead ball era hitters for my Hit List. I was always jawing with Joe Cronin, who had a broad knowledge of players from his era and before. And I still talk occasionally with Musial and DiMaggio and Mantle and Berra and an all-star lineup of other former major leaguers. They all have strong opinions — opinions that can't be ignored.

I know that my choices are not necessarily the same as yours, and that I'll never succeed in converting some of you to my way of thinking. Sure, I have some significant advantages when evaluating the talent of this and other eras. Hell, I was right there on the field for much of it and saw many of those guys up close. For well over 50 years I've been steeped in the practice and the lore of hitting. For many of us, however, rankings are devised as much in the heart as in the head. While I tend to be purely analytical when ranking the great hitters, there is an emotional element at work when people defend their favorite choices, and God knows those choices are none the less valid for that. Perhaps you saw Mickey Mantle electrify a Yankee Stadium crowd by hitting a tape-measure home run one warm summer day when you were safe in the crook of your father's arm — one of those days when all was right with the world. Or it could be your Italian heritage that caused you to worship the great Joe DiMaggio, although just watching him go from first to third on a single would be enough for me. That was a thing of beauty. Remember that great little book by Hemingway, *The Old Man and the Sea*? The old fisherman, Diego, liked DiMaggio because he had read somewhere that Joe's father was also a commercial fisherman. If you have a common bond of experience, the best statistical evidence in the world won't change your mind.

Maybe your ancestors hailed from Krakow or Warsaw and those Polish ties caused your pulse to quicken whenever Stan Musial or Yaz strode to the plate. It could be anything — a steadfast loyalty to a particular player's era or team or hometown can inspire your choices. That's the way it should be, and it doesn't have to be analyzed or defended.

Still, it always amazes me the way fans relate so strongly to a certain player, and the way those people come from all sectors of society. NBC sportscaster Bob Costas isn't ashamed to admit that he carries a Mantle baseball card wherever he goes. Conservative commentator and *Newsweek* columnist George Will puts aside weightier subjects to write an eloquent tribute to the batting consistency of Wade Boggs. Meanwhile, actor Dabney Coleman has written a nice piece in *Inside Sport* related to my hitting abilities, and his former TV persona, Slap Maxwell, used to invoke the spirit of Teddy Ballgame whenever he faced a personal crisis. It might have been a bit premature, but I appreciated the thought nonetheless.

Given this loyalty to particular players, it isn't surprising that argument is a big part of the allure of baseball. What was the greatest team ever? Who was the fastest pitcher? The slickest-fielding second baseman? Those kinds of questions are all fuel for the hot-stove league. But without a doubt the facet of the game that produces the loudest arguments is hitting. Who were the greatest hitters of all time? It's a debate that will continue to rage as long as baseball holds sway over the youth of this country, which I hope is for a long time to come.

This book will no doubt fuel a lot more argument. I hope it does. In fact, if it doesn't generate argument — and lots of it — it has probably failed in its purpose. Not that anything was deliberately done to cause such disagreement. No artificial controversy was built into the text to boost sales. I had my fair share of controversy in my playing days and I sure wouldn't go out of my way to create more at this point in my life. That's hardly necessary when everyone is so dead sure in his or her heart who the great hitters were — and who they were not. Still, baseball wouldn't be nearly as much fun if everyone cheered for the same heroes.

Let's face it, there has never been a perfect hitter. Ruth and Mantle struck out too much, and Cobb was a push hitter with no power. The two who would appear to have everything are Rogers Hornsby and Shoeless Joe. They didn't seem to have any real flaws, but I could point to every hitter *I* personally saw, including Ted Williams, and tell you where they fell short of their potential — *every* hitter I saw, including the greatest hitters I saw play. The only thing you can do is to investigate and find out who, for whatever reasons, made the best use of their talents.

That's why it's important for the reader to know that while this book is written from a hitter's perspective, and with a hitter's background and insights, it also incorporates a reliable statistical system to help validate each selection and assist us in the ranking of the top 20 hitters.

For comparison purposes, *Ted Williams' Hit List* used a publication called *Total Baseball,* by John Thorn and Pete Palmer, as our major source for statistical data. It's a comprehensive work and has served as our reference throughout this project. Not only does *Total Baseball* provide the more traditional statistics, such as batting averages, slugging percentages, home run and RBI totals, but it also features a smorgasbord of less traditional, but in many ways more revealing, stats.

Of those statistics related solely to hitting, I give special credence to one used by Thorn and Palmer, known as production. Production (PRO.) is determined by adding on base percentage (OBP) and slugging average (SLG.). On base percentage is a stat developed by Roth and Rickey in the early '50s. It is arrived at by calculating hits plus walks plus hit by pitch and dividing by at-bats plus walks plus hit by pitch. Slugging average, of course, is determined by dividing total bases by at-bats. We looked at various systems and methods, and we can't conceive of anything superior to this one. It is a simple statistic that is nonetheless as fair, as thorough, and as thought-out as any that has ever been used.

Production is the bottom line in hitting and that's why production is our bottom-line stat. It's a great indicator, a great yardstick of hitting. It also serves as an equalizer, a tool for making valid comparisons of hitters from various eras and for evaluating what a particular hitter has accomplished across his career. This single statistic most closely reflects my thinking on what makes up a superior hitter.

I realize that everyone has a different idea of what constitutes a great hitter. For some it's a high batting average. For others it's the guy with the most total hits — or home runs, or RBIs. I've *always* believed that slugging percentage plus on base percentage is absolutely the best way to rate the hitters. This is something I've been talking about for a long, long time. To begin with, I've always felt that the bases on balls factor should be given more significance in rating a hitter's overall performance at the plate. When I played, walks weren't counted nearly as much as they are now. Now they're starting to talk about it a little differently.

Even today, though, few people really realize the importance of those 125 extra bases. They only count the hits — the home runs and the doubles and triples. Well, let me tell you, a great hitter should walk three times for every strikeout. If a hitter like Don Mattingly isn't walking, he knows he's hitting too many pitchers' pitches. So I'm thrilled to see that they're finally starting to recognize the importance of the walk. I think it's overdue, you're damn right I do.

Total bases is the key. Production is the key. I have tried to take as my credo the belief that the *best* hitter is the most *productive* one. All you have to do to find the most productive hitters is start with the guys who get the most total bases and go from there. That's why the production stat is the best overall gauge of a hitter there is. It doesn't fail and it hasn't failed us.

Total Baseball actually carries it one step further to create a stat called adjusted production, which takes into account home park characteristics that help or hurt a batter, and league average. For our purposes I have ignored this variation, choosing instead to make those adjustments based on my own knowledge of ballparks, styles, and other, more subjective hitters' yardsticks. Some of these are very hard, if not impossible, to quantify, and you can't apply them to any neat formula, but I will speak in general terms later about many of those "compensating factors" that affect a player's performance. Hopefully they will serve to explain some of the apparent contradictions between the production numbers and the actual rankings.

In order to conduct any kind of fair comparisons, we must place the hitters on an equal footing. To the casual observer Pete Rose might appear to have an edge on Ty Cobb, because Rose sprayed out more base hits than any other player. However, when you consider that Rose was at bat almost 3000 more times than Cobb, and *still* finished his career with only 64 more lifetime hits, you start to see things a bit differently. Obviously it's important wherever possible to avoid comparing apples and oranges. On closer inspection Cobb was a bona fide Georgia Peach, while a Rose is a Rose is a Rose.

That's why one logical starting point is to measure accomplishments on a per-time-at-bat basis. I think that what a guy does per time at bat is very significant. You can never make me believe Mays and Aaron were better than Ruth and Gehrig and DiMaggio based on per times at bat. Mays and Aaron, and even Musial — and certainly Rose and Yastrzemski — are from an era of players whose careers weren't interrupted by service in the armed forces. They had a chance to carry on and play those extra four or five years, and then they started seeing goals that they could attain because of their longevity. And you sure have to say one thing: They had longevity! But when you start comparing them with the Ruths and Gehrigs per time at bat, it's right out the window with those guys.

Among those whose ranking was negatively affected by a limited number of at-bats was Hank Greenberg. Based solely on his production stats, Greenberg should have been fourth on our list instead of eleventh. However, Hank was only up 5000-odd times. Through no fault of his own, his career was cut short by the Second World War, and he was never the same after the war. So despite his great production numbers, I was compelled to move him down.

My ideal cutoff point for times at bat I would put at about 6500. Ideally, a guy would have to be up 6500–7000 times. Greenberg is a borderline case because of his time in the service. I lost four and one-half years of a career and I only got up 7700 times, so I can sympathize. Also due to unusual circumstances, Joe Jackson fell well short of 6500, as did Kiner and Mize. It's impossible to project what they might have done if they had played a full, uninterrupted career. They might have maintained those high levels throughout, or they might have started to fade anyway. Based on what I saw and heard about these individuals, I think they would have continued to dominate pitchers. But we'll never know.

We also gave considerable weight to the more traditional statistics. This explains another apparent contradiction. Some of Willie Mays' records — including production — are slightly more impressive than Aaron's. But Aaron hit more home runs than anyone else. That counts for a hell of a lot and has to be factored in. You can't ignore a feat like that. Those two guys were extremely tough to rank, but sometimes you have to go with your gut feeling and your own personal observations. In the case of National Leaguers, I often consulted former players from that league, guys who saw Mays and Aaron up close on a regular basis.

Mantle was another player who could well have been placed higher, except for what I saw as an unwillingness to make adjustments at the plate according to the count. With his talent, he might have been better than any of them. I really believe he had enough going for him: speed, power, the whole enchilada. I certainly have no hesitation in calling him the greatest switch-hitter who ever lived.

Batting averages were also considered. A lot of researchers will disagree, but to me an average tells you something, whereas a hit total can be deceptive because of varying numbers of at-bats. With few exceptions, anyone who doesn't hit .300 is not in *my* book, and is not a truly great hitter. I can't believe that he is. That's a pretty good rule to stick with. A .295 hitter would be considered at the 23rd, 24th, or 25th level — and then if you're not happy with someone else in there, you'd have to consider him. I would think that .300 would be about the lowest average, but that guy would get special consideration if he hit over 500 home runs. That was my rule of thumb, the glaring exceptions to my rule being Ralph Kiner and Mike Schmidt. But then Kiner, a lifetime .279 hitter, boasts the second-best home run frequency in baseball history, and Schmidt, a .267 hitter, hit 542 home runs and *owned* the National League pitchers for years. You can't ignore those considerations.

So an average is just another tool, and I sure don't consider a .300 average *in itself* as the criterion of who is the greatest hitter. There are countless numbers of high-average hitters who didn't come anywhere near the list: Carew, Boggs, and so on. But when you have all those other statistics — 1700, 1800, 1900 RBIs, 575 or 600 home runs, or at least 500-plus — *then* you've got to consider that guy.

Willie McCovey hit .270 lifetime, so, despite the 521 home runs, that — along with lower production figures — would work against him. And McCovey dominated the National League for several years. I have a lot of respect for him and he was damn close to making our list. Likewise, Ernie Banks wouldn't be considered because he was not a .300 hitter (.274 lifetime) and his production numbers were also relatively low — even though he hit 512 home runs and led the league twice. And we had to think long and hard about Mike Schmidt because he doesn't have an all-time-great batting average, even though he's a powerful hitter.

So almost all the guys we're talking about are .300 hitters. Maybe .298 is close enough for me, but not much lower, unless there are compensating factors which can't be ignored. I don't call Harmon Killebrew a great hitter: a great *slugger,* yes! You have got to mention him as a great slugger. And he *should* have been a great hitter. From where I stand, Killebrew and Banks should both have been greater hitters. They were great sluggers, but they should have been able to put it all together.

I don't pay quite as much attention to RBI totals because opportunity is what counts there. I had guys drive in as many runs as me who had 50 percent more chances to drive in a run, so it's deceptive.

The statistical criteria that we used to determine the top 20 hitters, therefore, include total bases and performance on a per-time-at-bat basis — in short, production. But as I've said, there are other considerations. You have to temper statistics with common sense and personal observation, otherwise you could list the top 20 production figures and close the book on the subject. Well, it ain't that simple.

Baseball is unique in a number of ways. Unlike football gridirons or basketball courts, no two baseball fields have the same dimensions, which obviously can have a huge effect on a player's offensive numbers, especially home runs. And then there have been changes in the ball, and in gloves and other equipment, which have had an impact on the efficiency with which the game is played. And night games and airplane travel and domed stadiums and artificial turf . . . an infinite number of factors that affect a hitter's performance and make fair comparisons especially difficult.

On the following pages I offer some thoughts on many of these compensating factors. I do this mainly by drawing on experiences from my own career, and I relate these personal anecdotes only to help illustrate the *kinds* of problems faced by hitters. Baseball is a flesh-and-blood game, and while statistics provide a standard of achievement, the game shouldn't — and can't — be reduced to a sterile numbers game. I hope that the point of view I offer will complement the wonderful research done by baseball historians.

THE BALLPARK FACTOR

What role do ballparks play in determining the success of a hitter? Did Home Run King Hank Aaron benefit from playing his career in so-called hitters' parks? Would I have been a better hitter, as some experts suggest, if I'd played in Yankee Stadium with its short right-field wall? Would DiMaggio, a right-handed batter, have produced better batting statistics in Fenway Park with that inviting Green Monster in left field?

Well, to begin with, I don't subscribe to the conventional wisdom that says DiMaggio and I should have switched parks, although I do think we would have done better in Detroit or Cleveland. How would I have fared in Yankee Stadium? I walked more times in Yankee Stadium than in any other place. For the 11 years that Casey Stengel managed the Yankee ballclub, there was a rule there that if Williams beats anybody in the seventh, eighth, or ninth inning, he'll get a fine. So you see, I didn't get as much to hit, although that's no excuse on my part.

I hit .305 in Yankee Stadium! And remember, I was walked more times in Yankee Stadium than in any other ballpark. Now back home at Fenway, I hit .365 against the Yankees lifetime, against the same pitchers, basically — but we had a pretty good supporting cast of right-handed hitters with that short porch to shoot at, so then those Yankee pitchers have got to pitch to you, and that made one hell of a difference. It's true that I had to hit about 400 feet at Fenway and about 310 in Yankee Stadium, but goddamn it, I had a hard time because I never got a very good ball to hit. As a result, I'd get at the plate in Yankee Stadium sometimes and just kind of relax and not really be ready and — Ball

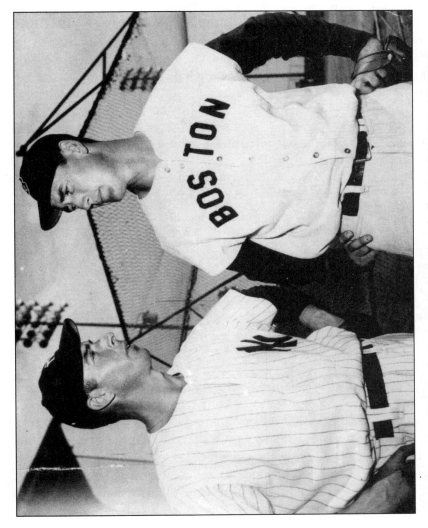

DiMaggio and Williams: the hottest rivalry in baseball.   AP/WIDE WORLD PHOTOS one! Ball two! — and heck, never get a pitch. And so I'd get lax sometimes. That's no excuse, it's the truth. You look and see how many times I walked in Yankee Stadium.

Hitters like Mel Ott are often criticized and their performance devalued because they played in friendly, and in some cases downright affectionate, ballparks. Statistics may not lie, but they don't always tell the whole truth either. Ott, for example, hit an inordinate 325 of his 511 home runs in a New York bandbox called the Polo Grounds where a 250-foot fly ball was a round-tripper. But give him his due. Ott was smart, too; he learned to adjust to his ballpark environment better than anyone else could.

The truly great hitters could hit anywhere, as indicated by this chart of DiMaggio, Mays, and Aaron:

	AB	AVG.	SLG.	OBP	HR	RBI	PRO.
DiMaggio:							
Home	3360	.315	.546	.391	148	720	.938
Away	3461	.333	.610	.405	213	817	1.015
Mays:							
Home	5239	.302	.567	.389	335	930	.955
Away	5642	.301	.549	.385	325	973	.934
Aaron:							
Home	5972	.303	.556	.382	385	1117	.939
Away	6392	.306	.553	.372	370	1180	.925

AB — At-Bats; AVG. — Batting Average; SLG. — Slugging Percentage; OBP — On Base Percentage; HR — Home Runs; RBI — Runs Batted In; PRO. — Production

If hitters were hired to design ballparks in the manner that Jack Nicklaus designs championship golf courses, what would they look like? Well, if I were the architect they would start with *damn* good lights. Good background. Sometimes at night you can have a better background than you have in the daytime. In some cases you don't really have to have a background at all at night because the lights are so well located. The Baltimore ballpark was terrible when the Orioles first entered the league. It was far better hitting at night than in the daytime, because there was a white school out there beyond the outfield, and their organization didn't do a damn thing about it. Just *terrible!* And I can tell you other ball-parks where the shadows get long and it gets tough. I'd rather hit at night in those parks.

We always had a pretty good background in Fenway Park. That's the reason people like to hit there. A lot of the parks had really good backgrounds: Detroit, Cleveland. Yankee Stadium, not so good. Of course, it always affects the visiting team more than it affects the home team. I can remember people saying that when there was a big crowd at Fenway, they thought the background was bad. It never bothered me because I was used to it, but with a left-hander pitching to a right-handed hitter, I know damn well it'd be tough.

A good hitter has to adapt himself a little bit to where he's playing. For instance, Vic Wertz played for Detroit, which has a short right field. He crowded the plate. We used to crowd him, pitch him high and tight, and he'd miss and swing a little late and get out. Every once in a while he'd crank one, but he wasn't a good hitter at that point. Then they traded him to Cleveland.

Cleveland was a bigger park, harder to hit in, and when he got there he must have said to himself, "No use in me trying to pull the ball. I'm going to get off the plate." And he became a hell of a hitter — a *hell* of a hitter! — hitting the ball a little more away from him and not trying to pull it. He sparked Cleveland to a pennant in 1954. Later he came to our ballclub and he was still a hell of a hitter. It just goes to show that hitters have to adjust not only to pitchers and counts but also to the unique character of the ballpark.

Everyone always thought that Griffith Stadium in Washington was a tough park to hit in. Well, hell, I loved to hit in Washington! The ball flew out of there and it looked like I was hitting downhill all the time. Some parks hit you in a different way. I always thought that the damn pitcher looked four feet closer to me in Philadelphia's Shibe Park than in any other place — but still I used to hit like hell there. In fact I went six for eight in Shibe Park to clinch .400 on the last day of the '41 season, so obviously I liked the place.

Another thing. You've got to make the home run distances *reasonable!* There are things in every ballpark that make it a little uncomfortable or that make it enjoyable, but most importantly you've got to be able to see the ball and you've got to have the fences reachable. Don't give the pitcher that much advantage. Hell, he doesn't need *that* much advantage. He's got eight guys out there and you don't need to have the fences 400 feet in every direction. I'd say down the line 335 feet, through the middle alleys 380 feet, and centerfield 405 to 410 feet. Now those are reasonable distances, but you've still got to hit the ball well for it to go out.

Domes are a necessary evil, especially in those major league cities with less temperate climes. I suspect that Montreal and Toronto both qualify — although it gets pretty cold in Detroit and Chicago and they still play outside. However, indoor or out, the dimensions must be fair. The big fault of domes is that most of them are not designed well for baseball. Houston, for example, was hurt, and will be hurt forever perhaps, and may even end up leaving the Astrodome, because the place isn't as fair a facility as it should have been. They have the fences located where Babe Ruth couldn't hit one out, and they've made a pitcher's *paradise* out of it. They may have straightened it out some now, though. Apparently the Seattle and Minnesota domes are both easy to hit in.

THE PITCHING FACTOR
Impact of the Slider

They talk about the slider as if it's a new invention that only the modern hitters have to struggle with. I started in 1939 and the slider was first thrown in 1947, so for about eight or nine years of my 22-year span in the big leagues I didn't have to face the slider, but I had the slider all the rest of those years. It really started to take over in '47, and in '48 certainly it was prevalent. Hell, yes — and from 1948 on I looked for the sliders, and I keyed my hitting on them.

I knew I could hit a fastball with anybody, but because every pitcher started to add the slider to their repertoire, I had to make that adjustment. Why? Because it was harder for me to hit the slider if I was looking for a fastball, harder to pull it and really get it in the air, than it was for me to look for the slider and adjust to the fastball and get *that* pitch in the air.

I really didn't give a damn if I hit it to right field. As long as I hit it good, I knew I could hit it out: left center, centerfield, or wherever the hell it was. So I had a much better chance of doing that if I was looking for the slider. And another thing. Looking for a slider made me wait a little longer, because the slider is a little slower pitch. If I'd keyed on the fastball and then gotten a slider, I'd be sure to hit a ground ball, and I sure didn't want to do that. Ground balls were *nothing* to me! They were *outs*! They had the defense stacked against me and they had all kinds of exaggerated shifts devised to stop me — and I sure couldn't beat anything out with my speed. From second base to home I had average speed, but when I took a good hard rip at the ball I'd fall toward third, and so I had a disadvantage going down the line to first. Those are all reasons why I decided to key on the slider.

A slider just gives the pitcher a third pitch, like in the old shell game. You can take *two* walnuts, and the guy gives you the fast moves with the walnuts and you don't even have to look, and you pick a walnut and you'll be right 50 percent of the time. But you put that third walnut in there and then you start guessing, because you don't know where it is. Your chances of guessing right immediately go down to 33 percent. That's why, for batters, the advent of the slider made a huge difference. If a pitcher relies on two main pitches, you're guessing right 50 percent of the time. What the hell, you may get five pitches in a given at-bat. All you've got to do is get one good pitch and guess right and get it in the right spot, and you should hit it pretty well. A good, experienced hitter will lay for it and jump on that one good pitch he sees. When you add the slider to the mix, your odds drop by a third and the pressure is really on to cash in on that one pitch.

So that's what the slider did. It gave every pitcher another pitch. It's not a curve, it's not a fastball, it's a slider. It's easy to learn how to pitch, and easier to control than a breaking ball. So right away that put another thing in the pitcher's arsenal. The impact on hitters was so great that ten years later they finally had to do something to try to help them, and that's when they dropped the pitching mound.

Mays called it the toughest pitch he faced; so did Aaron. The hitters were really suffering, and you know what happened when they dropped the mound? There were a couple of records set in the league, and everybody was hitting about 30 points higher right off the bat. That's how big an impact one phase of the game can have on hitters.

Those are all things that baseball fans should keep in mind. All those changes and refinements had an impact on hitters. Just as the fans should know that the lively ball was introduced in 1920. Ruth couldn't have hit 50 home runs in the dead ball era. The year he jumped from 11 home runs to 29, and then to 54, that signaled the advent of the lively ball era and changed baseball from a game of finesse to a game of finesse and power. The introduction of the slider was another one of those checks and balances that keep the batter or the pitcher from getting the upper hand.

The Forkball

Today pitchers make much more use of the forkball. It's become a reliable pitch for many of them. There were always guys who had some success with it — Elroy Face was one — but the big thing about the forkball is that it's hard to get it over the damn plate. And a 102-mile-per-hour fastball is hard to get over the plate! The wonderful thing about this game is that there are so many compensating factors. The guy with the tremendous exploding curve can't get the darn thing over and the guy who doesn't have all that stuff can thread a needle. The guy with all the power in the world can't make contact and the guy who has wings doesn't have power.

The Spitball

Should the spitball be legalized? No. I think that it's dirty and the pitcher doesn't need it. I think those illegal pitches are more of a psychological factor than anything else. I think many hitters psyche themselves out. For some of them it's just an act to let everyone think they are psyched out, because they can't hit the damn thing anyway. You know those guys, wailing and moaning after striking out. It's a handy excuse.

The big thing is, they see all of those trick pitches, and you know what happens? They swing at bad balls all the time. Anything that's that hard to throw or is that good is also hard to get over. But they still swing at them. There is no question about it: the modern hitter swings at an awful lot of bad balls.

Pitchers: Ted's Personal Gallery of Greats

Different types of pitchers give trouble to different types of hitters. I can only speak for myself and offer some examples of pitchers who were damn tough on *me*. They were usually the smart pitchers, like Whitey Ford, Bob Feller, Hoyt Wilhelm, Bob Lemon. They all had different strengths but they all had that in common.

New York Yankee Spud Chandler was tough on me. He was like Cleveland's Bob Lemon. He had a hard sinkerball and kept the ball down. He was a little herky-jerky, had a good curveball — a real quick curve. He was a hard guy to pull for a left-hander. And of course Lemon was very close to the same type of pitcher.

You know a guy who should have been as tough as any of them? A guy named Donovan, Dick Donovan, but he went too much with that one pitch, the slider. He had a better slider than either one of those other guys, and he had as good a curveball as either, and darn near as good a fastball, but he went with that one pitch too much. Some pitchers do that. Donovan won 20 games one season, but he should have been a more consistent pitcher.

The Yankees' Whitey Ford was tough on me. Hell, he never struck me out, but I never felt that I could ever really rip on him. He always had the ball down and away, down and away, down and away — and then POP — he brought it in on you. Then down and away again. He had a good, quick little curve. He was a good little pitcher. And then you take guys like Wilhelm, Lopat, a fellow named Scarborough who had a tough, hard curve. Those kinds of pitchers are still around today and still darn successful. Smart, crafty guys like Jimmy Key with the Yankees. Key looks real good to me. He would have been tough on me. He's a left-hander and he's got a good delivery, a tough, high, three-quarter delivery.

For speed I'd single out Trucks, I think. Virgil Trucks and Bob Feller were the Roger Clemens and Randy Johnson of that period. You say them in the same breath for speed. But when you talk about the greatest pitcher, there's no question: it has to be the Cleveland Indians' Bob Feller. He had a hell of a curveball. Herkyjerky. He was the kind of fellow that when he came into town everybody got geared up, because they knew they were going to see *Mr.* Feller. I think when you say that, you can see he had a great influence on the players of the day. They were going to see

Feller, something a little extra was going to happen that day. And it always did.

At that time they pitched differently to me than to anyone else on the Red Sox club. I would see the first knuckleball the opposing pitcher had, or the first screwball, or the first slider. A guy would come back to the bench and he'd say, "Goddamn, that guy threw me a slider." And I would be saying to myself, "Hell, he threw them to me last year!" Or a knuckleball, or anything else. They used to try things out on me, experiment on me. The big hitters always get that kind of special attention from pitchers. It's like a challenge for both of them, a showdown — gunfight at the OK Corral.

I once struck out on a knuckleball and everyone on our bench laughed. A little pudgy Cuban guy who smoked big cigars was pitching — I can't remember his name. Hellfire, he threw me three great knucklers and I swung and missed and I struck out. My teammates were all kind of laughing. We had a good lead, but I said, "Don't laugh, that S.O.B. is tougher than you think." They didn't know anything about him. But they soon found out.

I used to watch all these opposing pitchers in the bullpen. They were always playing around and experimenting. They show you what they've got in the bullpen because they want to throw everything they've got and work on certain pitches and all the rest. I was well aware of those pitches a lot of times. I can think distinctly of Detroit, where I was in left field and they'd be warming up out there, and I could see them and see everything that was going on. So I had a pretty good insight as to the type of pitcher a guy was. That's what good hitters have to do if they want to stay ahead of the game.

THE BAT, THE BALL, AND THE MODERN HITTER

Corked Bats

Blaming corked bats too much for the increase in hitting is just wrong. It's insignificant. They caught Cleveland's Albert Belle a while back and made a big deal of it. Let me tell you something: they are trying to make a lot of excuses for a goddamn lively ball. The big thing is, you can hit with a piece of banana wood or you can hit with a piece of dynamite, but you've still got to make contact and you've got to hit it on the good part of the bat. I think this business of the corked bats is way, way, *way* overexploited and bellyached about. Hellfire, it doesn't mean a thing. Now if the ball has been tampered with, that's a different thing.

Lighter Bats

Everybody asks why the hell I was so quick with the bat. I was pretty strong, not beastly strong, but mainly I was quick. You know why I was so damn quick? I want to tell you something: I had the lightest bat in the league for maximum strength per pound. And it started a trend toward light bats.

I had to laugh because in 1960 someone in the media brought up the fact that all of a sudden everybody's hitting for higher averages and all the rest of it. Willie Mays came out and he said, "Well, I have a lighter bat this year." And I thought, Well isn't that funny? Old Ted had it 22 years before. As Casey Stengel would say, "You can look it up." Today's players use much lighter bats.

Cobb used a heavy bat, a 40-ouncer, but even he made the move to a lighter model later on in his career. Ruth used barge poles, though! Some of his bats were 50 ounces or more. Musial's were about like mine.

On Patience

So many guys are swinging when they leave the bench. All you do when you do that is hit the pitcher's pitch, and don't you think the pitcher knows that? The pitcher says, "Hell, I'm not giving these guys anything to hit till I have to." So what's happening? The batter's getting something tough all the time.

The thing is, I always got criticized for taking a pitch an inch or an inch and a half off the plate. Nowadays when hitters do that they've got "great patience." And yet they were always lambasting me. Cobb got on me for that. And why Ty Cobb would do that I don't know except that he was a strange guy.

Now when they first asked me to compare Boggs and Mattingly, I said they have to give the edge to Mattingly because he hits 25 home runs and Boggs is hitting about seven. But Boggs is a better hitter any day — day in and day out. In my estimation Mattingly has gone back as a hitter. He's starting to give it that little curl and he's not very smart as a hitter. Boggs is a pretty smart hitter. He makes the pitcher pitch. If he's fooled, he doesn't fool with the pitch. When he's got two strikes, he'll go inside-out, inside-out. He has that great facility of hitting with two strikes. He doesn't strike out much. He's right there all the time. Not only does he concede with two strikes, he concedes with one strike, and that's why he doesn't hit the long ball. But then again, we're not talking about those guys for this list.

The Modern Hitter

It's easy to criticize the modern player. I always said I wasn't going to criticize the modern player. The only real criticism that I've ever leveled at Boggs or Rod Carew — outstanding hitters, outstanding hitters — is that in batting practice, Boggs will put a hell of a long ball show on for you in the bleachers, but in a game — phip! phip! phip! — he just tries to spray the ball. Well, batting practice and a game are exactly the same! You gear yourself up a little bit and, hell, if you can hit those balls in practice, you should be able to hit them in the game. And yet it doesn't happen. Don't ask me why.

That would be my only criticism, because they have already proved they can do it and yet they don't try. With two strikes, of course let 'em do it that way, but when you've got the count in your favor, when you've got a certain kind of pitcher, when you've got the wind, when you've got the park, when you've got the game on the line — the type of game where you want to try to crank one — do it!

I thought Boggs was capable of 20 home runs a year and I thought that George Brett was capable of 20 home runs a year (and that's when he wasn't hitting them). Carew hit 20 one year and never hit that many again. The only year Boggs did it was when they livened up the ball a couple of years ago and he hit 24 homers, in 1987. Since then he's only hit ten or 12.

Some readers might question the scarcity of modern day players on the Hit List. All I can say is that they were examined with the same scrutiny as the older players, and the rules for them today are the same as the rules for those guys then. They have been rated according to the same guidelines.

THE GEOGRAPHY OF HITTING:
THE RUSSIANS AREN'T COMING!

A few years ago, the Canadian hockey establishment and the NHL made the mistake of underestimating the Russians as an emerging hockey power. The Russians have also produced some pretty fair basketball players. But you can bet your ass they will never become a baseball threat, despite some growing interest in the sport. You can bet it won't amount to anything.

Their weather's lousy as I understand it. Cold. You could play three months of the year at most. There is no way you are going to compete against kids playing nine, ten, or even 12 months of the year in other countries. No way, *no way!* Why? Because the single hardest thing to do in sport is hit a baseball, and the way you excel most prominently and most effectively is by being able to hit.

The reason there aren't more Canadians in the major leagues is that — as I've said a million times — hitting a baseball is the hardest thing to do in sport, and in a place like Canada you get to hit only a fraction as much as I did when I played every month and every day of the year in San Diego. They have more time to play hockey and they're better at it than we are. But in baseball you need all the time and every opportunity to play and hit. So it's understandable that hitting is hard for Canadians and Russians.

That's why a little country like the Dominican Republic produces so many fine players. Their weather allows them to play a lot of baseball. Period. They are light and quick and and they gravitate to the infield where they cash in on that stuff. The Cubans are heavier and they produce more power hitters.

I don't know how you can make adjustments for cold weather. It's a pain in the ass and I never did like it. God, I hated cold weather. I couldn't get loose and I just didn't feel hitterish! It's just a hell of a lot tougher to hit when it's cold and it's a lot easier for the pitcher. He shouldn't get tired and he should be able to stay warm. And don't forget, when it gets cold you are usually hitting against a prevailing wind that's *always* blowing in.

That's why Harmon Killebrew's record is so impressive. Now he was a strong fellow, but he's from Idaho, for Pete's sake, with

Idaho's bad weather, and yet he hit more home runs in the American League than any other right-handed batter who ever lived.

It requires total commitment to overcome disadvantages like that! *That* is why people come out to the major league parks to see it done well. The hitters are what you talk about. Take Roberto Alomar, for example. He's a great little second baseman and he's fun to watch, but it's still the hitters that people pay to see; it's the hitters that they talk about on the drive home.

RUNS, HITS, AND ERAS

It would have been tempting to qualify the selections for the Hit List by dividing the choices into neat little compartments: best "dead ball" era hitters and best post-1920 "lively ball" hitters, or pre-1969 and post-1969. It certainly would have made the task much simpler, and in some ways it would have made for a fairer basis for comparison. But ultimately, I believe, it would have been a cop-out.

After all, when you talk about the great orators of history, you don't divide them into the pre- and post-television days, the Churchill era and the Kennedy era. When you rank the great singers of all time, you don't make allowances based on the style of music they played or the outmoded sentiments sometimes expressed in the songs. Surely greatness in sport, as in all things, rises above the eccentricities of a particular era, and a Cobb, Ruth, or Joe Jackson would have been a bona fide star in any era. Sure it was a different game, with different demands on the players. But the true greats were so talented and so driven that they could have adapted their skills to the conventions of any era.

One of the many great things about the game of baseball is the sense of continuity and history that it has carefully preserved. Unlike many sports, baseball is rooted in its history. The diamond heroes of yesterday are still revered and they provide the standards by which the next generation is judged. It's all connected and it's what makes baseball unique. Each generation of ballplayers adds another layer of accomplishment.

It's part of the rhythm of the game, the cadence of the game. If we set past generations apart as special cases, we're really saying

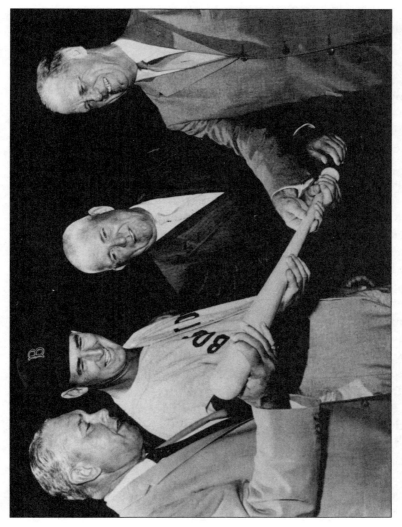

Terry, Williams, Hornsby, and Sisler: four members of the elite .400 club. NATIONAL BASE-BALL LIBRARY & ARCHIVE, COOPERSTOWN, N.Y.

that today's baseball is the genuine article and all that went before was just preparation. Well, I don't buy that. Sure every generation feels that its heroes were the real McCoy, but we shouldn't ignore the legends of the past either, because our children and grandchildren would then find it just as easy to dismiss the baseball heroes of the '70s, '80s, and '90s . . . and on and on.

So while it isn't easy to compare the Cobbs and Jacksons with the Schmidts and Aarons, my Hit List is a ranking of the greatest hitters of all time with no special conditions attached. And no apologies.

There's one other shamefully glaring historical fact that had a basic and profound influence on the makeup of my list. Until Jackie Robinson took the field for the Brooklyn Dodgers in 1947, blacks were denied the opportunity to show what they could do at the major league level. It's impossible to project what a hitter like Josh Gibson would have done against major league pitching, but based on eyewitness reports he was something to see. Who will ever know how many potential Aarons never got to show their stuff in the big leagues? As I said in my Hall of Fame induction speech, Gibson and other Negro League stars were robbed of that chance. I'm sure our list would look a bit different if the color barrier had never existed. Sadly we'll never know, and baseball is all the poorer because of it.

Having said that, it is appropriate and important to point out the watershed events that had a significant influence on the very nature of the game over the years and, by doing that, to put things in some basic historical context.

In the 1954 edition of *Baseball Stars* magazine, I discussed the practical differences between players of different eras in an article called "How to hit .400." In the time of Hornsby, Cobb, and Terry, I argued, there was

> **no night ball, no twilight-night doubleheaders, no one night stands and one day hops. The players of those days had a regular daily schedule. All his games began at 3:30 p.m. He was able to eat breakfast in the morning, lunch at noon and dinner at night. He didn't have to worry about playing under the hot sun**

one day and in damp heavy night air the next. When the game was over he could expect a normal period of relaxation and plenty of rest that night. It's not surprising that Nap Lajoie hit .405 in 1901; Joe Jackson hit .408 in 1911; Ty Cobb hit .420 in 1911, .410 in 1912 and .401 in 1922; George Sisler hit .407 in 1920 and .420 in 1922; Harry Heilmann hit .403 in 1923; Rogers Hornsby hit .401 in 1922, .424 in 1924, and .403 in 1925; Bill Terry hit .401 in 1930.

As I went on to point out,

It was the era of the dead ball, but it was a quick dead ball. Maybe it didn't go over the fence but it kept dropping over the infield for base hits. In 1911 Ty Cobb collected 248 hits but only eight went the distance. Frank "Home Run" Baker led the league with nine homers. In fact the entire American league collected only 193 homers, less than the Brooklyn Dodgers racked up in 1953. The lively ball no doubt increases the home run output but it is no boon to the batting average. The best proof is that in the very same year, 1911, the National League, for the first time, tried the livelier cork center ball, while the American League stuck to the standard "dead" one. Hans Wagner, the N.L.'s leading hitter, batted .344 to Cobb's .420, while the N.L. hit 314 homers.

I sounded almost envious when I talked about those good old days, especially that notorious year of 1930:

1930 was a great year for batters. Bill Terry hit .401. Thirteen National Leaguers and nine American Leaguers batted over .350. 93 players in both leagues hit over .300. Those fellows were not "natural hitters," they were dedicated students of the art of hitting. They practiced hitting before and after the game. They knew all about the different woods. They knew as much or more about opposing pitchers than their managers. They became students of meteorology. They studied the winds and the air currents. They made a study of pitching mounds in every ball park. They spent hours watching the pitchers for telltale signs, what they threw, how they threw, whether they tipped their pitches. They lived and dreamed baseball. That was their way of life.

I went on to contrast the "simplicity" of the dead ball era with problems hitters of the fast-paced '50s faced in their quest for the magic .400:

Suppose it's Sunday. You play a doubleheader in New York, rest awhile and have dinner at 8. You find you have to play the next day under the lights in Boston so you get on a sleeper, breakfast on the train and eat dinner at the hotel between 3 and 4 o'clock in the afternoon. You're at the ballpark by 6, loggy after the meal, but you feel better at 8 when the game begins, though the air is damp and heavy, there's dew on the grass, and a chill wind comes up. The game ends at 11, you grab a sandwich, and hit the hay at 2 a.m. Between 10 and 11 next morning you arise just in time to have breakfast and dash out to the park for a game which starts maybe at 1:30, or maybe as late as 3. No wonder a really great hitter like Joe DiMaggio never cracked the exclusive .400 circle.

Boy, the more things change the more they remain the same. I'm sure Ty Cobb and Harry Heilmann were complaining about how easy it was for Honus Wagner and Hugh Duffy and all the guys who came before them too. It's almost laughable. Sure the game has progressed and society has changed, training methods are superior and all of that, but in the end I think it all evens out. There were pressures in the dead ball era, there were different pressures when I played, and today's players face a whole new set of problems and pressures. Some things have been made a lot easier for them and some are probably tougher too. In the end, though, a hitter still has to prove himself at the plate, and a truly great hitter would stand out in any era. You can just bet a smart guy like Tyrus Raymond Cobb would be able to make adjustments to his swing and terrorize the pitchers of 1995, just as he did those poor sods back in his own era.

BASEBALL'S GENERATION GAP: A BRIEF HISTORY

Nonetheless, it's important to be aware of some of the milestones in the chronology of baseball and how they affected hitting:

• From the turn of the century to 1910, the baseball, featuring a rubber center, can best be described as dead.

• In the 1910 World Series, a cushioned cork center was introduced, enlivening the ball. In 1911 American League averages soared 30 points over the previous year; Ty Cobb batted .420. The NL homer king stroked 21, compared to 10 for the previous year's winner.

• In 1920 the ball was dramatically enlivened. .400 seasons became commonplace and home run totals soared. Ruth had 11 homers in 1919, 29 in 1920, 54 in 1921, and 59 in 1922.

• In 1930 the baseball was once again juiced up, this time for one season only. It still allowed ample time for Hack Wilson to stroke 56 homers and drive in a record 190 runs before becoming a mere mortal the following year with 13 HRs and 61 RBIs. Bill Terry hit .401 in 1930. He was the last National Leaguer to reach that mark, but three other senior circuit batters hit better than .380 that year, and the overall league batting average was a lofty .303.

• Over the years there have been a number of other developments which have produced varying and perhaps cumulative effects on hitting. Night baseball (1935), domed stadiums (1965), artificial turf (1966), lowering the pitcher's mound (1969), changing the strike zone (1969), expansion of the major leagues (1961, '62, '68,

'77), and the advent of air travel have all had an impact. These represent the natural growing pains of the sport, however, and have altered the fundamental nature of the battle between pitcher and batter very little.

THE PHILLY FACTOR

There's another factor that plays a role in the creation of the great hitter, and it has nothing to do with on-field performance: the media. Players who perform in the spotlight in New York or Los Angeles tend to get more attention and coverage than those in smaller cities like St. Louis or Atlanta — at least before Ted Turner and CNN turned that Georgia city into a media mecca. Hank Aaron in Milwaukee and Atlanta got much less ink than Willie Mays in New York and San Francisco for precisely that reason. Players like Frank Robinson would have been major stars if they had played in New York instead of Cincinnati and Baltimore.

Both Al Simmons and Chuck Klein, one a member of my Hit List and the other a near miss, are classic examples of this phenomenon. Both performed in Philadelphia, and their feats went largely unnoticed outside the Keystone State. W. C. Fields' headstone supposedly reads, "I'd rather be here than in Philadelphia." I think maybe those hitters could appreciate why he felt that way.

Honorable
Mentions

TEN WHO CAME CLOSE

The following ten hitters came closest to cracking the Hit List:

HITTER	AB	AVG.	SLG.	OBP	HR	RBI	PRO.
Chuck Klein	6486	.320	.543	.379	300	1201	.922
Bill Terry	6428	.341	.506	.393	154	1078	.899
Dick Allen	6332	.292	.534	.381	351	1119	.914
Hack Wilson	4760	.307	.545	.395	244	1062	.940
Duke Snider	7161	.295	.540	.381	407	1333	.921
Willie McCovey	8197	.270	.515	.377	521	1555	.892
Willie Stargell	7927	.282	.529	.363	475	1540	.892
Harmon Killebrew	8147	.256	.509	.379	573	1584	.887
Goose Goslin	8656	.316	.500	.387	248	1609	.887
Earl Averill	6353	.318	.534	.395	238	1164	.928

Some of those on my Honorable Mention list came very close to making the top 20, and I agonized over some of the choices right up to the last minute. In the end, however, it's important to differentiate between great hitters for average, great sluggers, and those select few who combined both facets of hitting. Some of those on the Honorable Mention list were great sluggers and some were great hitters for average, but few were both.

The slugger is a power hitter who sacrifices getting on base by striking out more in his pursuit of the long ball. As a result, some of these guys' low on base percentages play a major role in their not making our top 20. On the other hand, some great "average" hitters failed to make the Hit List because they did not hit for power like they should have. In Bill Terry you've got a .400 hitter, for Pete's sake, who is not in our top 20 because he failed to hit home runs during the lively ball era. A lot of his contemporaries hit marginally more homers than Terry did in the '20s and early '30s. And Terry's career roughly paralleled Babe Ruth's, while Ruth hit 560 more homers than Terry under similar conditions. It's one thing for Honus Wagner to hit only 101 homers over a 21-year career in the dead ball era, but it's quite another to fail to hit the long ball in the lively ball era.

The greatest hitters are those who succeeded in combining slugging and hitting for average. It's not necessarily true that you have to sacrifice one for the other. Look at Hornsby, and Foxx and Gehrig. If you've got the ability to get the bat on the ball, then you can still take care of yourself pretty nicely after two strikes, so why not take advantage of what you've got on a given day? There may be a pitcher on the mound who looks like he's throwing you beachballs. Why not take a little liberty and go for the downs against that guy? Boggs and Brett are both good examples. They both could hit with two strikes. You've got to concede with two strikes, but hell, Boggs concedes all the time.

With some pitchers I faced, I'd say to myself, "I don't care if he has *two* strikes on me," I was still looking to hit the long ball. I might have to hit a tougher pitch but I wasn't worried about that against certain guys. (Of course, against *some* pitchers I didn't want *any* strikes against me.) A great hitter should be able to assess the situation and hit accordingly. The 20 hitters on my Hit List, to a greater degree, did it all!

Following are thumbnail sketches of Chuck Klein, Bill Terry, and Willie McCovey, three who came close to cracking the list.

Willie McCovey

Career: 1959–1980

Bats: L   **Height: 6'4"**   **Weight: 198**

Willie McCovey was one of the most feared sluggers in the National League. It's difficult to believe that a 6'4" giant known as "Stretch" could play in anyone's shadow, but for most of his career that was the case with McCovey. For 14 seasons McCovey played alongside that other Willie, the legendary "Say Hey" Kid, Willie Mays. Comparisons were inevitable and the charismatic Mays usually got the bulk of media attention. The fans in San Francisco loved McCovey, though, because he was one of their own, whereas Mays had brought his show in from New York when the franchise was moved west.

McCovey led the National League in home runs three times, in 1963 with 44, in '68 with 36, and in '69 with 45. In 1969 he was a one-man wrecking crew, batting .320 and driving in 126 runs to capture the league MVP award. He finished up with 521 home runs, the same number as me.

Willie McCovey absolutely dominated his era. In many ways he was certainly a more feared hitter than Mel Ott, who made our list and gets so much more attention. McCovey played for 22 years and did a lot despite a low .270 average.

Bill Terry

++
Career: 1923–1936

Bats: L   **Height: 6'1 ½"**   **Weight: 200**
++

Bill Terry was the last National Leaguer to hit .400. He batted .401 in that great hitters' year, 1930, equaling Lefty O'Doul's 254-hit record in the process. Despite his slugger's proportions Terry was a classic line-drive hitter. His .341 lifetime average is second only to Rogers Hornsby among National League hitters. Starting in 1927 the big left-hander put together a string of ten consecutive .300 seasons. He accumulated six 200-hit seasons and six consecutive 100-RBI campaigns.

They used to write that Babe Ruth was my boyhood idol. That's not true. As a kid I never really idolized anyone, but the closest thing to an idol that I had was Bill Terry. Now why was that? I was born in 1918, and in 1930 Terry hit .400, when I was 12 years old — and you know that's an impressionable age. That's the only reason I can think of for it. I look back now and I think, that son of a gun hit .400, and I did it too. It's almost eery. I told Bill Terry about that one time. He was well liked by his teammates and fellow players but, like me, he wasn't a darling of the press.

Terry was a rough old fellow too. He was brutally frank — some would say arrogant. He certainly had a competitive drive. In 1933 he fanned the flames of an already bitter rivalry between his Giants and the crosstown Dodgers. Apparently he was asked about the pennant chances of the Dodgers and responded by asking, "Are they still in the league?"

Bill Terry: the last National Leaguer to hit .400. BETTMANN ARCHIVE

Terry was smart, an intelligent hitter. But he was also really well liked, a born leader, as his later managerial career suggests. "Memphis Bill," as they called him, led the Giants to three National League pennants during his years at the helm, winning the World Series in 1933. After his retirement those baseball smarts translated into financial smarts, as Terry parlayed his bravado into big money in the oil business.

He used to chew me out because I wouldn't go to the Hall of Fame induction ceremonies every year. I *never* used to go to Hall of Fame functions. I was inducted and then I moved right out of town. I should have stayed there and enjoyed myself and had a hell of a time; but I didn't. Bill Terry convinced me that I was missing out on a lot.

I still haven't changed that much in that regard, despite what everyone might think, but I do appreciate things a little bit more now. I appreciate being with those old guys — great, great players. And they treat you like royalty. Hell, they treat you so well that you even think you *are* pretty good when you get out of there.

When Terry hit .400 in 1930 it was the lively ball era, and Babe Ruth had hit 60 home runs just three years earlier. And yet, Terry was never a power threat, managing a meager 154 homers throughout his 14-year career. And he only had 1078 RBIs. That's why there was some wavering on his selection to the top 20, and why he was ultimately left off.

I never saw him play, but Cronin said that he was a great hitter and his record certainly indicates it, although his limited number of at-bats might be another negative factor.

His .340 average puts him in the top echelon, and a .400 season puts him in a hell of a bracket! You can't dispute the fact that there are very few hitters who have the statistics of Terry. In some ways his career parallels Heilmann's, even though Heilmann had superior production numbers .

Despite the fact that he had his greatest years when baseball averages and baseball production were the highest in the history of the game, Bill Terry was certainly one of the greatest hitters. Not in my top 20, though; let's say the top 25.

Dizzy Dean was an overpowering pitcher and completely fearless on the mound. The Hall of Famer had an
Achilles' heel, however, when it came to Bill Terry. One
afternoon, after Terry had sent three batted bullets past
Dean's head, Pepper Martin decided it was time to offer
his teammate some advice. "Diz," he remarked, "I don't
think you're playing Terry deep enough."

Chuck Klein

Career: 1928–1944

Bats: L   Height: 6'   Weight: 195

K lein was another guy who was given a lot of consideration for the list. He was a great hitter, but like Al Simmons he played in Philadelphia and was forgotten about. He got no respect and he deserved much better.

Chuck Klein was one of the premier hitters at the beginning of the lively ball era. He had every advantage in the Baker Bowl, which was his home park for most of his career in Philly. It was a little bandbox of a ballpark and it probably helped him to hit 300 home runs, but it doesn't take away from his talent. You have to take advantage of every opportunity that presents itself, and Klein certainly did that.

During my whole life as a hitter, I sought out the knowledgeable people in baseball and grilled them about hitting. I was always asking questions and I could be fairly persistent, not to say relentless. In all that time I never heard one guy who didn't say that Chuck Klein was a hell of a hitter. Even though I didn't really see him play, all the other hitters in the National League loved his hitting.

He really exploded onto the scene in 1929, his first full season. That year he hit .356 with 145 RBIs and a league-leading 43 home runs. He won the home run title four times and the batting title once, with .368 in 1933. In 1930 he joined the league hitting parade with 40 homers, a .386 batting average, and 170 RBIs. Significantly, he didn't lead the league in *any* of those categories in that notorious year — which should tell you something.

Chuck Klein: four home run titles and one batting championship.

He won the MVP award in 1932 with 38 homers, 137 RBIs, and a .348 mark, and for an encore he won the Triple Crown in 1933 with 28 HRs, 120 RBIs, and a .368 average. Not surprisingly, those five years were the best he ever managed. If he could have sustained those numbers over his 17-year career, they'd have to build an extra wing on the Hall of Fame to house his memorabilia.

My only reservation about Klein was that he didn't dominate the league for an extended period the way, for example, Mike Schmidt did during his career. Still, 300 home runs and a .320 average can't be denied.

When Chuck Klein was traded to Chicago for a brief two-year stint in the midst of his career, his offensive statistics fell accordingly. Without the Baker Bowl advantage, he was merely mortal.

SOME WHO SHOULD HAVE BEEN BETTER

Some people will say that I'm too critical of hitters, and certainly it bothers me when a young player comes into the Majors loaded with natural talent and doesn't live up to his potential. Sometimes those guys turn out to be fine players, and some have even made it to the Hall of Fame, but to my mind they could have been even better.

Sometimes, of course, fate intervenes, and through no fault of his own, a player is robbed of the opportunity to show what he can do. Here are some notable hitters who fell just short of their potential for a variety of reasons:

• Carl Yastrzemski — Yastrzemski was a grinder, and I saw that when I first went to spring training with him. I said, "Boy, this guy is all coiled up. He's like a spring." And you can read where I said that if you want to look it up. I said that I liked his intensity. Yaz was an

Yaz and Ted: together they stroked 1073 home runs for the Red Sox.
AP/WIDE WORLD PHOTOS

experimental guy with his style, with his bat. He could never convince himself what was good and when he was doing it right. And he couldn't convince himself when something was wrong. He changed a lot. Hell, at one point he had his hands way up in the goddamn air. How are you going to swing from there? I told him that as an opposing manager with Texas when he was in a bad slump. "First, get your hands down." And then finally, before he quit, I was up with the Red Sox, helping them with spring training, and he said to me, "Ted, I'm going to drop my hands," and I just said, "That's good."

Yaz wasn't as smart as he should have been. Let me give you an example. The Red Sox were playing the Yankees in that 1978 playoff game where Bucky Dent hit the home run to win it for New York. The Yankees had Ron Guidry, the crafty little left-hander with the great fastball, pitching for them. Guidry had a fine year with a 25–3 record and a microscopic 1.74 ERA that year. He was a good little pitcher with a good hummin' little fastball, and he also threw a good slider.

Before the game Yastrzemski came up to me and he said, "I'm going to look for this guy's slider today." "Bullshit," I said. "Look for the fastball. Hit the fastball."

First time up Carl got a home run on the fastball. Now you can talk to Yastrzemski and say that he's getting jammed and now he should look for the slider. Cripes, they've been throwing fastballs to him all day long, and sure Guidry might still come back with it, but he's almost guaranteed of a slider if Guidry's whistled a couple of fastballs by him. But he was still thinking fastball and he popped up to end the game. He didn't know how to make those adjustments during the game. That's just one concrete example of his baseballic thinking. It shows a tendency, a lack of proper thinking.

I never played with Yaz, but Bobby Doerr said he had the best single year Bobby ever saw, and Bobby played with me for ten years! In 1967 Yaz had a great year: he hit 44 home runs, 121 RBIs, and a .326 average to win the Triple Crown. That shows you the kind of talent he had and what he was capable of doing. He did everything for the Red Sox that year: if they needed a clutch hit or a stolen base, he got it; if the situation called for a ninth-inning home run, he hit it; if they needed a great game-saving catch, he made it. For that one year, he was

Babe Ruth, Ty Cobb and Honus Wagner rolled into one. But one year doesn't do it. Yaz had desire and he had a great body and he had longevity. And I've told you what he was missing as a hitter. He wasn't as smart as he should have been, and he never knew when he was doing it right.

• Pete Reiser — You might not have heard quite so much about Stan Musial if Pete Reiser hadn't gotten hurt, because Reiser was a switch-hitter who could run like hell, hit .343 in his first full season in the big leagues, and was a super player. He might have given Musial a run for his money over in the National League. He just might have been a better player than Musial or Rose or anybody over there.

A lot of people who saw him in his first couple of years thought he was the best player in the league. Then fate intervened and he became a victim of his all-out style of play. He ran into the fence four or five times. He practically knocked his brains out once. Then he knocked them out again, and at the end he was getting almost punchy.

He hung on for ten seasons and finished with a .295 average, but he could have been a great one. He was a coach when I came to the big leagues, and by God, I had a lot of respect for him.

• Joe (Ducky) Medwick — Medwick was another guy who was a hell of a player and got hurt. The difference was that he put up some great numbers before he got hurt. His statistics indicate that he deserves some consideration, even though they were dragged down after the injury.

He won the Triple Crown in 1937 with 31 homers, 154 RBIs, and a .374 average. His slugging percentage that year was .641, so you've got to respect that guy. He finished his career with a .324 average, but he was never the same after his injury.

• George Brett — Physically, Brett had all the tools to be a glorious hitter, but in his mental approach to the game he always lacked something for me. I certainly don't consider him an outstanding hitter. He's one of those guys who might not always have been as serious about the game as he could have been.

• Fred Lynn — Lynn had so much going for him when he came up to the Red Sox in 1975. I only wish something could have motivated him a little more — but he was a hard guy to motivate. Nothing stirred him up. He was content to have a pretty good year and go to the beach. He didn't have that little extra, despite his natural talent. He didn't have what Yastrzemski had: intensity.

You hate to see those young guys blowing the one chance they'll have. In 25 years they'll say, "Well, God, I wish I'd done just a little bit better." But that's life. I can look back on my own career and have regrets.

• Goose Goslin — Goslin was a hell of a hitter, according to Joe Cronin. Now I know he must have been good, but whether Cronin was quite right putting him in the same category as Lou Gehrig — and that's just what he told me — I don't know. Joe told me that, so you've got to believe he was in the same category as Gehrig for sheer *talent*. But there's nothing to indicate that from the records. Goslin hit .316 lifetime with 248 homers and only led the league in hitting once, with .379 in 1928. That's a far cry from Lou Gehrig.

• Al Kaline — I used to talk a lot about hitting with Kaline when he came up. He had everything to be an outstanding player. He led the American League in hitting in his third year, 1955, with a .340 average, but he never led it again. Now something has got to be wrong there. Either he didn't catch up with the pitchers or the pitching finally caught up with him. That sure doesn't take away from his accomplishments, though. He was an all-round player who hit .297 lifetime with 399 home runs and was elected to the Hall of Fame. That ain't bad.

• Yogi Berra — Berra was a talented all-round player and one of the best-loved people in the game, but you can't put him on a list of the great hitters. His predecessor with the Yankees, Bill Dickey, was a better hitter than Berra, but Yogi was still a fine little hitter. He swung at some bad pitches, but not the bad low ones, only the bad high ones. And he was strong: he could get the ball in the air and really hurt you. It was hard to get the ball down to Berra. He never led the league in any major category but still hit 358 home runs and batted .285 lifetime.

• Charlie Gehringer — Gehringer was an early candidate for the list but he only hit 184 home runs. You've got to consider that: he's a .325 lifetime hitter but he didn't hit many home runs. A good hitter ought to hit a home run at least every 20–22 at-bats — somewhere between that and Ruth's once every 12 times up.

So you look at Gehringer and he falls a little short in the real power department. He also played in a friendly ballpark; Navin Field in Detroit was a hell of a hitter's ballpark.

• Pete Rose — He was a bear-down son of a bitch and I'd want to have him on my team. He was a great all-round player, and you've got to give him high marks for his hustle and his attitude. But frankly, I didn't like his hitting at all. Rose had no power. You know what Mantle said about Rose? He said if he hit like that, he'd wear a skirt. Mantle's a rare bird who speaks his mind, and I agree with his analysis. There's no reason Rose couldn't have crashed a few more homers. When a guy gets the count in his favor, why not crank up and try to rip one? Rose seldom did. He was the first singles/doubles hitter to make the big bucks, and that was his trademark.

• Ernie Lombardi — Lombardi was a guy who could flat-out hit. He couldn't run a lick, and yet he still batted .306 lifetime and actually led the National League in hitting in 1938. Look his record up and I think you'll be impressed.

There isn't anyone who saw Lombardi hit or who played with or against him who doesn't say, "He was as good a hitter as I ever saw." He finally got in the Hall of Fame, but it was a long time coming.

• Wade Boggs — Red Sox coach Ralph Houk asked me about Boggs in the spring of '82. I said, "He'll get the bat on the ball as well as anyone," and I was sure proven right there. I always thought that Boggs was capable of hitting 20 home runs a year, but except for 1987, when they livened up the ball and he hit 24, he's content with 10 or 12 per season. He has great bat control, but there's more to being a great hitter than that.

• Rod Carew — In 1977, when Carew looked like he was making a run at a .400 season, *Sports Illustrated* put the two of us on the cover. Carew didn't quite make it, finishing at .388, but he was a superb hitter for average throughout his career. Rod had a ton of ability but, as outstanding as he was, he could have been even better. He averaged less than five home runs a year and he was capable of many more than that. When I asked him about it he said, "That's the type of hitter I am." Well, he hit 14 twice. Why didn't he come back and do it again? He was good enough to do much better in the power department.

• Andre Dawson — Dawson was a terrific young hitter. Like Eddie Murray he was underrated as a hitter; both were outstanding. I liked Dawson's style. Unfortunately he has bad pins and it hampered a great career. There was a time when I'd have considered Dawson a franchise player.

• Reggie Jackson — What a hell of a guy to have in your lineup! He was a threat from the time the game started until the final out. He has to be considered one of the very best clutch hitters in the game's history. He's certainly been one of the great Fall players of all time; they didn't call him Mr. October for nothing. His World Series stats are incredible. He must like the cold weather because he's done some job in the Fall Classic. He struck out an awful lot, but when he connected he made things happen.

• Jim Rice — He hit as if he had two strikes on him all the time. He was as strong as a bull, but he was swinging when he left the bench. When you do that you hit the pitcher's pitch — and if you don't think the pitcher knows that, you're fooling yourself. He just says, "Hell, I'm not giving this guy anything to hit until I have to." The result is that you're hitting something tough all the time.

• Dave Winfield — He showed me that he was a fine player. At first I didn't think he could hit, but I was wrong, he *could* hit. He finally got his feet on the ground. I don't know how he straightened himself out, but he's a smart individual and I guess he figured it out. He realized how the pitchers were working him and he caught up with them. I respect a guy like that.

• Dave Parker — I was never impressed with him. A great big guy like that and he got more dinky little hits than anybody else I ever saw. How many home runs did he end up with? 328 in 18 seasons. He had a few fairly good years — but not good enough. I mean, the guy was 6'5", 230 lbs, ran well, and he had several sub-20-homer seasons. I wouldn't call that great.

• Harmon Killebrew — Killebrew had more home runs in the American League than any other right-handed hitter in history. He was a strong mother! I remember they used to ask me who would turn out to be the better hitter, Killebrew or the other Twins outfielder, Bob Allison. I said, "Boy, I think Killebrew. I think he has a better swing," even though at the time Allison was probably considered a little better, because he swung down on the ball and made a little more contact. But not nearly as many good things happened as when Killebrew swung.

• Roger Maris — He didn't have overwhelming career statistics but in 1961 he did something that has never been done by anyone else before or since: he got 61 homers in a single season. Somewhere along the line, they are going to have to recognize the fact that he hit those 61 home runs and that he did it while playing alongside one of the greatest players of all time — Mister Mantle. I would be inclined to think that Maris deserves to be in the Hall of Fame.

The Hit List

Ted Williams' Hit List

Rank	Hitter	At-Bats	Batting Avg.	Slugging Pct.	On Base Pct.
1	Ruth B:L	8399	.342	.690	.474
2	Gehrig B:L	8001	.340	.632	.447
3	Foxx B:R	8134	.325	.609	.428
4	Hornsby B:R	8173	.358	.577	.434
5	DiMaggio B:R	6821	.325	.579	.398
6	Cobb B:L	11,434	.366	.512	.432
7	Musial B:L	10,972	.331	.559	.418
8	Jackson B:L	4981	.356	.517	.423
9	Aaron B:R	12,364	.305	.555	.377
10	Mays B:R	10,881	.302	.557	.387
11	Greenberg B:R	5193	.313	.605	.412
12	Mantle B:R&L	8102	.298	.557	.423
13	Speaker B:L	10,195	.345	.500	.428
14	Simmons B:R	8759	.334	.535	.380
15	Mize B:L	6443	.312	.562	.397
16	Ott B:L	9456	.304	.533	.414
17	Heilmann B:R	7787	.342	.520	.410
18	Robinson B:R	10,006	.294	.537	.392
19	Schmidt B:R	8352	.267	.527	.384
20	Kiner B:R	5205	.279	.548	.398
/	Williams B:L	7706	.344	.634	.483

Home Runs	At-Bats Per H.R.	At-Bats Per Strike Out	Runs Batted In	At-Bats Per RBI	Prod-uction
714	11.76	6.32	2204	3.80	1.163
493	16.23	10.14	1990	4.02	1.080
534	15.23	6.20	1922	4.23	1.037
301	27.15	12.04	1584	5.16	1.038
361	18.89	18.49	1537	4.44	1.010
117	97.73	21.06	1937	5.90	.945
475	23.10	15.76	1951	5.62	.977
54	92.24	26.48	785	6.35	.940
755	16.38	8.94	2297	5.38	.932
660	16.49	7.13	1903	5.72	.944
331	15.69	6.15	1276	4.07	1.017
536	15.12	4.74	1509	5.37	.979
117	87.14	35.90	1562	6.67	.927
307	28.53	11.88	1827	4.79	.915
359	17.95	12.30	1337	4.82	.959
511	18.50	10.55	1860	5.08	.947
183	42.55	14.16	1552	5.06	.930
586	17.08	6.53	1812	5.52	.929
548	15.24	4.44	1595	5.24	.911
369	14.11	6.95	1015	5.13	.946
521	14.79	10.87	1839	4.19	1.116

STATISTICALLY SPEAKING

I didn't want *Ted Williams' Hit List* to be a dry statistical analysis of what I think is the most exciting and uniquely human facet of baseball, but I did want to be able to back up my insights with some hard and fast truths. The statistical categories employed in this book and on the chart on page 85 represent traditional yardsticks of excellence such as batting averages, home run and RBI totals, slugging percentage, on base percentage — and production, one of the newer statistics developed to allow for a more fair and complete standard of hitting excellence. Here is a brief glossary of statistical terms.

On base percentage, a statistic developed in the early '50s, was refined and adopted by major league baseball in 1984. Following the lead of Thorn and Palmer in *Total Baseball*, I have omitted sacrifice flies from the equation for purposes of greater accuracy. On base percentage (OBP) is obtained by calculating hits plus walks plus hit by pitch and then dividing by at-bats plus walks plus hit by pitch.

Slugging percentage is arrived at by dividing total bases by at-bats. A home run, for example, represents four bases, a triple three, and so on.

Production is the sum of on base percentage and slugging percentage. *Total Baseball* describes it as "a simple but elegant measure of batting prowess, in that the weaknesses of one-half of the formulation, On Base Percentage, are countered by the strengths of the other, Slugging Average, and vice versa." As I pointed out earlier, I have chosen not to use the PRO./A (production/adjusted) refinement that mathematically factors in home park dimensions and league averages. I have decided instead to let my knowledge of these and other factors be my guide.

1 George Herman (Babe) Ruth

††††††††††††††††††††††††††††††††††††††

Career: 1914–1935

Bats: L   **Height: 6'2"**   **Weight: 215**

††††††††††††††††††††††††††††††††††††††

is record says it all. Babe Ruth is the greatest hitter to ever play this game and the most famous athlete who ever lived. I was tempted to refer to his real-life exploits as Bunyanesque, but you could just as easily call Paul Bunyan's feats Ruthian. Now *that* tells you something about the man: when you talk about those two American legends the terms are practically interchangeable. The difference is that Bunyan was a fictional character while Ruth actually *did* those things, and while fact and fiction may become a bit blurry when people talk about the Bambino, the cold hard facts are enough to place him in a league by himself.

No wonder America loved Ruth. He did more for baseball than probably any other individual. He was easily baseball's most significant figure. He brought it back after the Black Sox gambling scandal, and he rejuvenated the game. He was a tremendous drawing card, a charismatic type of individual who was just perfect for the job. The game of baseball pretty near catered to what he could do. They livened up the ball. They built Yankee Stadium because of him. They did everything.

Who's to say he wasn't the greatest? I don't know. Cripes, he was certainly the greatest power hitter this game ever saw, bar none. They say he borrowed his swing from Shoeless Joe Jackson.

EXCLUSIVE — COPYRIGHTED PHOTO
GEORGE LYONS
ONLY PICTURE EVER TAKEN IN UNIFORM
FIRST MEETING OF

I personally think that Babe Ruth has to be the greatest player of all time.
GEORGE LYONS

Wherever he got it, he went on an offensive rampage that will never be touched. He couldn't run that well — he looked more like a sumo wrestler than a ballplayer — but he still hit .342 lifetime. He owns the major league record for the highest slugging percentage in a season, with .847 in 1920 .847! He "dropped" to .846 the next year. His 714 lifetime homers stood as the all-time record until Aaron broke it in 1973. He hit 50 homers four times and 40 or more 11 times. His total of 60 round-trippers remains the record for a 154-game schedule.

The very fact that Ruth hit so many more home runs per time at bat than other hitters puts him in a class by himself. A home run every 12 times up is almost unbelievable. Ruth led the American League in homers 12 times, and he holds a *lifetime* slugging percentage of .690, the best by far.

I personally think that Ruth *has* to be the greatest player of all time, and I'll tell you why I think that. He was not only a great slugger — the greatest slugger the game has ever seen or ever will see — but also a great pitcher. I know we're talking about hitters here, but you can't ignore the fact that he was one of the best pitchers of his time. He compiled a 94–46 win-loss record with a skimpy 2.28 ERA. They'll never make me believe that he was a great outfielder, but all the old-timers will tell you that he did a good job: never threw to the wrong base and all that stuff. And he played right field in Yankee Stadium, which is a tough field to play. More importantly, he resurrected the game with his allure for the fans and his flamboyant style of play. And his hitting! I'm damn sure the fans didn't come to see Ruth play right field, they came to see him hit. And he never disappointed them.

He had such magnetism about him, and he was the guy with all the slugging marks. Ruth dwarfed everybody during his day, and the great players of the time all looked in awe to him. These were Ruth's contemporaries, guys who had fought tooth and nail to beat his hated Yankees, and still he was the man they all looked up to as the draw, as the game itself — or at least as the savior of the game. Eddie Collins was a great player himself — a Hall of Famer — but when he talked about Ruth he talked about him with reverence. Looking back, it's not much of an exaggeration to say that Ruth saved the game of baseball. When the Black Sox scandal threatened to destroy the integrity of the game, it was Ruth who led the national pastime out of its darkest hour and into a new era of popularity. He had those gaudy statistics, and he was an outrageous kind of guy. He had a zest for life and a kind of roguish charm that captured the imagination of the American public. Hell, he changed the very nature of the game by moving the focus from finesse to power. You know, they call it a game of inches — and it certainly was for his contemporaries — but it was usually transformed into a game of 500–600 feet when Ruth came to bat.

During the so-called dead ball era, he hit more homers than anyone ever before. Then when the ball was enlivened in 1920, he exploded for 54 round-trippers, more than any single American League *team*.

I read a book in which Ruth talked about hitting, and he said it pretty near the way I would say it. He described it a little differently, just like some of these guys today are saying things differently than I did in *The Science of Hitting*, but he certainly indicated that you had to have a good ball to hit and all the rest. What he said I liked and I agreed with.

I only met Ruth once, at an exhibition game in 1944 when he was 46 or 47 years old. It was for some charity. He still had that fluidity to his swing but he was pretty fat by then, and I remember that he hurt his back that day swinging the bat. It must have been 106 degrees in the shade, and he and some other old-timers were drinking beer throughout the game.

Even today the name Ruth is synonymous with baseball and, especially, with hitting. He played his last major league game more than 60 years ago and you can *still* hear kids in school yards taunting their friends with, "Who do you think you are, Babe Ruth?" Hell, his name is as well-known now as it was when he played. You can't say that about any other American athlete.

Appropriately, Babe Ruth hit the very first All-Star game home run. It was a two-run shot at Comiskey Park in Chicago in July of 1933. Babe's American Leaguers won 4–2 over the National League's best.

BALLPARK FIGURES: Yankee Stadium, "The House that Ruth Built." Left field was 280.58' in 1923, and 301' in 1928. Deep left center was 460' in '23. Centerfield was 490' in '23. Deep right center was 429' in '23. Right field was 294.75' in 1923, and 295' in 1930.

2 Lou Gehrig

HHHHHHHHHHHHHHHHHHHHHHHHHHHHHH

Career: 1925–1939

Bats: L   **Height: 6'1"**   **Weight: 212**

HHHHHHHHHHHHHHHHHHHHHHHHHHHHHH

abe Ruth epitomized the power and the glory of the Yankee dynasties, DiMaggio represented Yankee style and class, and my friend Mickey Mantle exemplified rawboned Yankee talent. It took Lou Gehrig to put all those things together in one package. That's why he will forever remain the Pride of the Yankees. To me it's much more than just a catchy Hollywood title.

The courage that Gehrig showed in facing the disease that bears his name, and that eventually took his life, is the stuff of legend, but long before that he proved that he was something special — a man of iron. He played in 2130 consecutive games from June 1, 1925, to April 30, 1939, before finally asking to be taken out. Until that fateful day arrived, he went head to head with teammate Babe Ruth, and not only held his own but in some phases onfthe game even managed to surpass the Babe.

You look at Babe Ruth and you look at Lou Gehrig and you say to yourself, "Hell, there's no difference between the two. They're about the same." And they were! How in the world a team could have a one-two punch like that, I'll be a dirty son of a gun if I know — although some guys have come close for a season, maybe. In recent years the Oakland A's came pretty close with their two big guns, Canseco (since traded to Texas) and McGwire. They are not as good hitters, of course, but they're tough hitters, big strong guys who had a lot of other guys around them who could wear you out. In the early '60s Mantle and Maris also did it

I don't think any player could match Lou Gehrig if Gehrig could have played out his career in good health. NATIONAL BASEBALL LIBRARY & ARCHIVE, COOPERSTOWN, N.Y.

for a year or two. But Ruth and Gehrig did it throughout their careers. That's the difference.

In 1927 Gehrig hit 47 homers and was still outdone by Ruth, who picked that year to hit 60. Still, with the exception of Ruth, I don't think any player could have matched Lou Gehrig if Gehrig could have played out his career in good health. Only God knows what he'd have done. His statistics are so close to Ruth's in every way, and still he was up barely 8000 times (8001 official at-bats). Some of these guys are up 13,000 times and *still* haven't managed as many home runs as Gehrig.

When you think of Ruth and Gehrig, how the heck can you separate those two guys? They were both .340 hitters. They both slugged .650 or .600, and Gehrig didn't loft the ball as much as Ruth but he sure as hell hit it hard. He hit screaming liners. And he was a faster runner than Ruth. He stole home 15 times in his career, and I can't picture Ruth doing that.

Gehrig was the son of German immigrants who knew about the importance of education. He attended Columbia University on a football and baseball scholarship, and I'll tell you, there weren't very many college guys in the game at that time. He graduated to the Yankees in 1923, and his 17-year career stands as a monument to consistency. He led the American League in home runs three times (one tie), in RBIs five times (one tie), and in batting average once.

A two-time MVP, he set the American League record in 1931 for most RBIs with 184, a total that even the Babe couldn't match. In 1934 he captured the Triple Crown with a .364 average, 49 homers, and 165 RBIs.

Gehrig's lifetime grand-slam total is really incredible. He came through in those clutch situations a record 23 times. For 13 straight years he drove in more than 100 runs and *averaged* 147 RBIs during that span. He once hit four homers in one game, and for 12 consecutive seasons he blasted more than 20 home runs per season, averaging 38. That's a barrage! No wonder they called him the Iron Horse.

In the 1932 World Series he led the charge with a .529 average, three homers and eight RBIs in a four-game Yankee sweep of the Chicago Cubs. He did all that damage in only 17 trips to the plate.

In 1938 Gehrig's statistics started to wane just a bit. His batting average dipped below .300 for the first time since his first full season, and he hit "only" 29 home runs and drove in 114. People thought he had a bit of an off year, but they sure didn't expect that it was the beginning of the end.

I still remember that one game that Gehrig played against me in 1939, his last year as a Yankee. I was a rookie with the Red Sox, and I remember he hit a humpbacked line drive to me his first time up and grounded out the next time. I seem to recall that he swung down on the ball a bit, but he still had amazing power. I remember following him up the stairs to the field a couple of times that day . . . a raw rookie following the great Lou Gehrig up the steps . . . and I remember thinking that he looked pretty good — not great, but pretty good even then. Of course, I didn't know what he was facing at the time. He quit just eight games later and was almost immediately named to the Hall of Fame.

On July 4th of that year 61,000 fans jammed into Yankee Stadium to pay tribute to Gehrig. He responded with that memorable speech in which he said, "Today I consider myself the luckiest man on the face of the earth."

Can you imagine what desperate thoughts must have gone through pitchers' minds when they had to face Ruth and Gehrig on a hot afternoon at Yankee Stadium? He was a great hitter. So great that he was able to play alongside the most flamboyant figure in the history of American sport and still emerge as a star in his own right.

The 1927 Yankees, featuring Babe Ruth and Lou Gehrig, is often called the "greatest team ever." Ruth hit a record 60 homers, led the American League in runs scored (158), bases on balls (138), on base percentage (.487), and slugging average (.772). But it was Gehrig, with 47 homers and a league-leading 52 doubles and 175 RBIs, who was chosen league MVP that year.

BALLPARK FIGURES: During Gehrig's inspired career Yankee Stadium offered up the following targets for the left-handed slugger. Left field was 280.58' until 1928, when it expanded to 301'. Deep left center was 460' until 1937 when it became 457'. Centerfield was 490' in 1923 and shrank to 461' in '37. Right center moved from 429' in '23 to 407' in '37. Right field was 294.75' in '23 and 295' in 1930.

3 Jimmie Foxx

f you asked the baseball gods to design the perfect power hitter, they would probably just point to Jimmie Foxx and say, "It's already been done." When you talk about power, you start with Foxx and Ruth. Foxx carried on where Ruth had left off. He inherited the long ball mantle that the Bambino had created. If anyone was ever capable of actually tearing the cover off the ball, it would be Double X, my teammate when I first came to the Red Sox. They called him The Beast, but really he was just a big gentle Maryland farm boy with bulging biceps.

Now Jimmie Foxx may not have been the most intelligent hitter I ever knew, but he certainly wasn't a dumb guy: he was smart at working a pitcher. Hell, he knew just how they were going to pitch, and he'd just lay for it, and when Foxx got his pitch he hit it like Mantle.

It sounded like cherry bombs going off when Foxx hit them. Hank Greenberg hit them pretty near as far, but they didn't *sound* that same way. They sounded like firecrackers when Mantle and Foxx hit them — and I never heard anyone say that about Ruth's or Greenberg's home runs. Foxx and Mantle were two guys from different eras, but I saw quite a bit of them both. I never saw a right-handed hitter, except Mantle and Foxx, really crush the ball — I mean *crush* it — when he hit it like those guys did. Killebrew could hit them hard at times, but I don't think it made the same sound. No, it might make a crack, but I always thought that

It sounded like cherry bombs when Foxx hit them. NATIONAL BASE-
BALL LIBRARY & ARCHIVE, COOPERSTOWN, N.Y.

Mantle's and Jimmie Foxx's sounded just a little different. They were both built the same. I've got to think that they both generated great bat speed.

I played three years with Foxx and he was toward the end of his career, but I do have to say that the year before I played with him he hit 58 home runs, so he wasn't too bad even when I got there. We were on a road trip in '39 or '40 and I had a chance to see Jimmie Foxx's last great performance as a hitter, and I'll always remember it. I was on second base and Mel Harder was pitching for Cleveland at Municipal Stadium, and he was really fooling everyone with his stuff. All day his pitches were either sailing or they were sinking. This was long before the Indians organization shortened the distances by installing those inner home run fences. Foxx hit a drive to left center over the 435-foot mark that went over the wall into the seats way, way back there. I mean, he hit it a ton.

After that we went to Detroit, and he hit one into the upper deck in the left centerfield bleachers, a mile back there. It was the longest ball I'd ever seen hit. Then we went to Chicago, and he hit a humungous home run over the left-field bleachers there. So I saw Jimmie hit three long home runs in three series in three different cities toward the end of his career. And I'll never, ever forget those home run blasts.

Back at Fenway I remember him hitting this long, long homer over the Wall into the teeth of a gale, and I remember looking at all those muscles as he trotted around the bases, and shaking that huge hand of his as he crossed the plate, and feeling almost weak. I was a skinny little guy anyway, and I felt weak in comparison to Jimmie Foxx.

For 12 seasons, from 1929 to 1940, Jimmie never hit less than 30 homers a season, and he *averaged* 48 homers during that period. He rang up 13 consecutive 100-plus-RBI seasons and maintained a career batting average of .325. That's a combination of power and average that is almost unheard of among modern-day hitters. Today they are either power hitters or hitters for average, but they are very seldom both.

Oh, Foxx was a hell of a player — and he was a very popular guy. He was a big old lovable bear of a guy. He could run pretty near as fast as Mantle, and he was built the same way. On the Red Sox we used to say, "Look at that son of a gun run." He would always talk about what he'd look for next time up. He'd say, "He'll give us that cheap curve," or, "I know he's going to bust me high and tight all the time." No detailed technical theories on the science of hitting, just a wealth of practical advice gained from years of experience. He was obviously good at reading the pitchers. Joe Cronin used to get me together with veterans like Foxx, Joe Vosmik, and Doc Cramer to talk hitting on those long train trips. Cronin realized that this would help to shake things up and get a young player like myself revved up. For an impressionable young hitter like myself, just being in the presence of a wily old veteran like Foxx was better than an all-day hitting clinic. It was like a tonic.

If production is the yardstick of the great hitter — and I sincerely believe that it is — then Jimmie Foxx must be the Henry Ford of hitters. Hell, he had production numbers that would have made Lee Iacocca envious.

Pitching ace Lefty Gomez once faced Jimmie Foxx in a key situation at Yankee Stadium. Time after time Lefty continued to shake off catcher Bill Dickey's signs. Finally the exasperated Dickey made a trip to the mound and demanded to know just what pitch the future Hall of Famer wanted to throw. "Nothing," replied Gomez. "I figure if I wait a while, maybe he'll get a phone call."

BALLPARK FIGURES: Foxx spent his career in Philadelphia's Shibe Park and Boston's Fenway Park. Shibe Park, where Foxx toiled from 1925 to 1935, offered the following test for the right-handed power hitter. Left field was 334' in 1922, changed to 312' in '26, and to 334' in '30. Left center was 387' in 1922, and moved back to 405' in '25. Centerfield was 468'. Right center was 393'. Foxx's second home (1936–42), venerable, angular old Fenway, featured a 37' wall known as the Green Monster just 315' away in left field. Left center was 379' beginning in 1934, and deep left center extended to 388'. Centerfield was 468' in 1930, and 388.67' in '34. The deepest corner, just to the right of dead center, was 420' in 1934. Right field was 332' in 1936, 322' in '38, 332' in '39, 304' in '40, and 302' in '42.

4 Rogers Hornsby

++++++++++++++++++++++++++++++++++++++

Career: 1915–1937

Bats: R   **Height: 5'11½"**   **Weight: 200**

+++++++++++++++++++++++++++++++++++++

ogers Hornsby can lay legitimate claim to being one of the greatest right-handed hitters of all time. They called him the "Rajah," and his career began in the dead ball era, but it really sprang to life, along with the ball, in the 1920s. He came very close to being the perfect hitter, if such a creature exists.

Starting in 1921 he averaged an incredible .402 over a five-year span, and in 1924 he achieved the highest average in the modern history of the game, hitting .424. His .358 lifetime mark is second only to Ty Cobb's .367, but unlike Cobb over in the American League, Hornsby also featured power in his offensive arsenal. In fact he led the National League in homers on two separate occasions and hit over 300 round-trippers throughout his career. What a combination of power and average!

Hornsby was one of my coaches at the Red Sox farm team in Minneapolis when I first came up. He was one of the most knowledgeable guys I have ever talked hitting with. Here I was, a 19-year-old kid, and he *wanted* to talk about hitting all the time. Boy, I sure took advantage of the opportunity to pick his brains. And Hornsby was a smart hitter too. He gave me the most positive advice when I asked him, "What do I have to do to become a great hitter?" He couldn't have been nicer, and I'll always have a warm spot in my heart for him. Hornsby's advice was this: "Get a good ball to hit." That was it! He said you've got to get a good ball to hit. So that wasn't even *my* golden rule (as espoused in *The Science of Hitting*).

Hornsby came very close to being the perfect hitter — if such a creature exists. NATIONAL BASEBALL LIBRARY & ARCHIVE, COOPERSTOWN, N.Y.

Actually, I'd already had that rule but without knowing how important it was. I walked a hundred times in the Pacific Coast League at 18 years of age, and I walked 150 times in Minneapolis at 19, so you know I *instinctively* got a good ball to hit. Then I got a little stronger, kept getting a little better, and all of a sudden I was cranking them a little better. Now they were a little more afraid of me and BOOM, BOOM, BOOM. Hell, I was a young, skinny, 155-lb kid at 6'4", but as I got stronger and I got better and I got more experience — BOOM — it all fell together. When I got to the majors, I realized that was the best advice Hornsby ever gave me. It gave me a foundation for my hitting career.

Hornsby used to stay after practice almost every day while I hit. He was almost 50 at the time but he was still as keen as mustard. You have to think that all that time I spent around him had an impact on me. We used to have little contests — line drive hitting contests — and I'll tell you he could still sting them even then.

I looked up Hornsby and you can look him up too. I said to myself, you know, Hornsby hit all the time in St. Louis. He was a right-center hitter, and right center in the Brown's ballpark (Sportsman's Park) was 365 feet away. It was a cozy ballpark for him. That's where Musial hit too, but Hornsby — *whew* — just hit them out there. He could hit them all over, but he was a right centerfield hitter to a great degree and the park really helped him. And he could run like a deer.

Now in addition to all these pluses, the ground is harder than rock in St. Louis, so the balls went through right field like a rocket. So I said, "Goddamn, no wonder he hit so good!" Well, he got in trouble with principal owner Sam Breadon of the Cardinals and they traded him to the New York Giants. He had just gotten through hitting .424, .403, and .317 in St. Louis and they traded him to New York (in 1927) with those Death Valleys in right center and left center. You know, he hit .361 that year, so he could hit anywhere! You can't deny his accomplishments by pointing to the cozy dimensions of his ballparks in places like St. Louis and Chicago. The record book shows that he hit .359 at home during his career and .358 on the road. That should close the book on that subject.

Hornsby captured six consecutive National League batting championships and led the senior circuit in slugging percentage nine times. In 19 of his 23 major league seasons he batted .300 or better.

In 1937, he cracked a dramatic pinch-hit homer to right field at Fenway — way, way back there in the deepest part of the ballpark. They were still talking about it five years after I came up to Boston.

Hornsby had an abrasive nature, and he was always criticizing DiMaggio — and he even got to criticizing *me* about what he saw as my refusal to hit to left field to foil the Lou Boudreau shift. He wanted to know who DiMaggio thought he was when he was asking for $27,000 a year in just his third year in the majors. Joe had just got through hitting 46 home runs with 167 runs batted in, and had batted .346, and Hornsby wanted to know who the hell this guy thought he was! Well, the greatest player I saw, that's who he was. After seeing up close what DiMaggio could do with his bat and his glove over the years, I made up my mind right there and then that I would never criticize a young player like that, because you just never know what they might end up doing. I almost did it with Mantle, but thankfully I didn't say it out loud.

So Hornsby wasn't overly diplomatic, and DiMaggio didn't like him, but Hornsby treated me as well as anybody could have treated me.

There are some similarities in our two careers. Hornsby and I remain the only two-time Triple Crown winners and we both came within a hair of winning three. He had great eyesight, and they always said that of me — although as I've said elsewhere in this book, my eyesight wasn't *that* good. And I guess you could say that we were both quite well respected and highly regarded by members of the umpiring fraternity because we very seldom questioned a call. I've read that Hornsby was so completely dedicated to hitting that he avoided movies and reading for fear that they would detract from his sharp eye at the plate. Hell, even I didn't go that far. It's funny because I like to think that a lot of young hitters have benefited from advice that Hornsby gave me and that I passed along in *The Science of Hitting.* Hornsby's advice would probably have been to save your eyes by not reading the book!

When Stan Musial was a household name in the '50s, former Cardinal owner Sam Breadon, the same guy who had feuded with

Hornsby and eventually traded him to New York, was asked if Musial was his greatest player ever. They say Breadon thought it over and replied, "No, I couldn't say that. There was Hornsby." That shows you how great the Rajah was.

Rogers Hornsby's keen batting eye was respected throughout baseball. Once, after three consecutive called balls to the Rajah, a brash young pitcher complained loudly to the umpire, only to watch as his fourth delivery landed in the distant bleachers. Hall of Fame arbiter Bill Klem patiently explained these events to the irate rookie. "When the ball is over the plate, young man, Mr. Hornsby will let you know."

BALLPARK FIGURES: Sportsman's Park was home to the right-handed Rajah for much of his major league career. Left field was reduced from 350' to 340' in 1921, was changed to 355' in '26, 360' in '30, and 351.1' in '31. Left center was 379'. Centerfield was 430' in 1926. Right field was 325', changed to 315' in 1921 and 310' in '31.

5 Joe DiMaggio

Career: 1936–1945

Bats: R 　　　　**Height: 6'2"** 　　**Weight: 193**

iMaggio was the greatest all-round player I saw. I give it to him over Mays simply because he was a better hitter than Mays. I saw him play, I saw what he could do, and I'm positive that he was a better hitter than Mays. He didn't have quite the power that Willie had, but he was certainly smoother, and he was a classic hitter. DiMaggio was a .325 hitter in Yankee Stadium, a tough ballpark, and he looked great doing it. At the plate he was poetry in motion; his fluid swing was a thing of beauty.

I can't say enough about DiMaggio. Of all the great major leaguers I played with or against during my 19-year career, he was my idol. I idolized Joe DiMaggio! The incredible thing about him is that his road record was even better than his home record at Yankee Stadium. Now, I had more home runs on the road than at Fenway, but DiMaggio was a better *all-round* hitter away from home. It just shows what a hell of a hitter he was. Still, in 13 seasons in New York he hit 148 homers in the Stadium, which is about 11 per season. He also owns the best home run to strikeout ratio in the history of the game, with 361 homers and only 369 strikeouts. That's a 1.02 ratio.

They were always making comparisons between DiMaggio and me. The sports pages were full of it in the '40s and '50s. It was a hotly debated rivalry, and the media tried to find feuds where there was only mutual respect. The consensus seemed to be that I was the better hitter, but that DiMaggio was the consummate

111

I idolized Joe DiMaggio. NATIONAL BASEBALL LIBRARY & ARCHIVE, COOPERSTOWN, N.Y.

ballplayer. I sure had no argument with that verdict. For me, hitting was always my first consideration. Everyone asks what Joe would've done in Fenway. Armchair managers dreamed of a trade between the Yankees and Red Sox. It was a switch that was supposed to help both Joe and myself, and our respective clubs. On paper I suppose it looked like a deal made in Heaven, and legend has it that it was briefly agreed to by Tom Yawkey and the Yankee brass one night. Both parties apparently thought better of it in the sober light of day.

Well, I'll tell you, I'd rather have seen DiMaggio in Detroit or even the Cleveland ballpark to break a record, because he could hit a ball well to centerfield and left center, but he could also hit a ball pretty well to right center. A good hitter can make accommodations to any ballpark, and that's what DiMaggio did, but he was not as good a hitter in New York as he'd have been in Detroit.

Basically Joe was a left-center, left-field hitter. We should have pulled shifts on *him* like they pulled on *me,* because he was a dead-pull hitter, and if he ever got one to the right of the shortstop. . . . Very few times have I seen him thrown out on a ball to the right of shortstop. He'd beat it out. That's how good he was going down the line. We never did throw him out.

Remember, I didn't say DiMaggio in Fenway, did I? Because that's a short porch, and he would have had a hell of a time getting a good pitch to hit. "The hell with him!" the pitchers would say, and they'd pitch him low and outside, low and outside — and all of a sudden he'd be hitting to no-man's land in centerfield. As a hitter, he'd be betwixt and between. He could pull the ball with anyone who ever played, but he'd have had it tough in Fenway because opposing pitchers wouldn't give him anything to pull. And against the Green Monster (Fenway Park's 37' left-field wall), he might not have hit so many home runs anyway, because DiMaggio was not a lofty-type hitter. He could hit the ball high, but it generally wasn't the Greenberg type of homer; it was the Foxx kind of homer, more BOOM, BOOM, more like hard, high line drive homers. The Wall might have turned some of thosw shots into long singles. So I think DiMaggio would have fared better in Detroit, and I think he'd have fared well in Cleveland at Municipal Stadium.

DiMaggio was a stylish hitter, the most stylish right-handed hitter I ever saw. And even if he didn't hit it well, he had a chance to beat it out. Against Joe, the infield was always playing back, and he got a chance to beat it out, because for a right-handed hitter he got away from the plate really well.

It's incredible to think that during DiMaggio's 56-game hitting streak in 1941 he never attempted a single bunt in 223 official at-bats. During that streak he batted at a .408 clip and showed some power with 16 doubles, 4 triples, and 15 homers. He won the MVP that year, although some people felt that I should have gotten it, because I hit .406 that same year. Well, I never felt I should have won it in '41! DiMaggio had an incredible year and led the Yankees to the pennant. There's no doubt that his streak was one of the most amazing feats in baseball history.

Joe captured the American League MVP award three times in all, in 1939, '41, and '47. He led our league in homers twice, in RBIs four times, and in batting average twice. He finished his career with 361 homers, a .325 batting average, and 1537 RBIs. He was named to the Hall of Fame in 1955.

There's no question that the two premier hitters in the American League for 15 years were DiMaggio and myself. But no one has greater admiration for DiMaggio as a hitter than Ted Williams. Joe DiMaggio could do it all. He hit the ball *hard*! Screeching line drives. He was smart and he was good. I was almost inclined to put him ahead of Hornsby as a great right-handed hitter, but you can't deny Hornsby's stats.

But Joe DiMaggio's career cannot be summed up in numbers and awards. It might sound corny, but he had a profound and lasting impact on the country. How many athletes can make that claim? Despite what Simon and Garfunkel sang about him, every baseball fan knows that DiMaggio could never really be forgotten. For many fans he's become baseball's knight in shining pinstripe armor. Hell, for some he was almost the embodiment of the American dream. In fact when that earthquake hit San Francisco during the World Series a few years ago, the commentators made references to DiMaggio's home as if it were the residence of royalty.

As far as I'm concerned, they weren't far wrong.

Marilyn Monroe, otherwise known as Mrs. Joe DiMaggio, returned from entertaining the troops in Korea with stories of the warm reception she had been accorded from 100,000 lonely soldiers. "Joe," she gushed breathlessly, "you've never heard such cheering!" "Yes, I have," the Yankee Clipper gently replied.

BALLPARK FIGURES: The right-handed DiMaggio played his entire career in New York's Yankee Stadium, a ballpark which seems much better suited to left-handed pull hitters. Left field measured 301' down the line, falling away to 402', 415', and 457' in deep left center; hence to 466' at the left of centerfield screen, 461' in centerfield, 407' in right center; and 295' to 296' in right field.

6 Ty Cobb

†††††††††††††††††††††††††††††††††††††

Career: 1905–1928

Bats: L   **Height: 6'1"**   **Weight: 175**

†††††††††††††††††††††††††††††††††††††

y Cobb was a man possessed of keen intelligence, blazing speed and unsurpassed batting skills. And I guess some would say that he sometimes played the game like a man possessed. Period. With all that he accomplished he should have been the quintessential American hero. Instead he is seen as baseball's eternal antihero. He had an all-consuming passion for perfection, and while it drove him to greatness on the field, it also helped to alienate him from teammates, opponents, and fans.

Cobb was the one and only. He was the greatest all-round player of his generation, and some of the old-timers will tell you he was the best of all time. He was certainly in the same league as Ruth for his contribution to baseball. There's no denying his greatness. Cobb hit .367 lifetime — the highest in the history of baseball — and no one will ever do it again. He was revered by his opponents. Even his severest critics had the greatest reverence and admiration for his talent. I think of all the players who ever lived — *every* player who *ever* lived — Tyrus Raymond Cobb was the fiercest competitor who ever walked on a baseball field.

I didn't actually see him play, but he was so intelligent, and at 6'1" and 175 lbs he was big for his day. And he was fast as lightning stealing bases. Put it all together: total bases, .367 average, sliding this way, sliding that way, stealing home! He did everything, so you *know* you had to respect Tyrus Raymond.

Tyrus Raymond Cobb was the fiercest competitor who ever walked onto a baseball field. NATIONAL BASEBALL LIBRARY & ARCHIVE, COOPERSTOWN, N.Y.

The Georgia Peach reached the coveted .400 mark on three separate occasions and captured a record 12 American League batting crowns. In 23 of his 24 seasons he batted .300 or better. Many of his batting and base-running feats will never be equaled. He stole home an incredible 35 times, and with that awkward — at least for me it would be awkward — hands-apart batting grip he racked up huge slugging figures. He hit those long doubles and triples in the so-called dead ball era. (I don't like that term, because it makes it sound like the ball was about as lively as a resin bag, whereas it was a quick dead ball from what I understand.) When Pete Rose finally overtook him in total hits in 1985, it was more a tribute to Rose's longevity than any serious challenge to Cobb's pre-eminence as the most prolific hitter of all time.

Just take a statistical snapshot of his career. It speaks for itself. He won nine consecutive batting titles from 1907 to 1915, batted .371 in 1916 and lost the title, and then won three more in a row. He accumulated 4190 hits and scored a total of 2245 runs, the most ever. But it wasn't just his hitting that made him such a devastating force. He was probably the most versatile and multidimensional of the players on my list. He won games in every imaginable way — and some you can't imagine.

Cobb was as intelligent a guy as I ever met in baseball. I always said that the two most intelligent athletes that I ever talked to — and I'd have to put Hank Greenberg in there as a very intelligent guy too — were Gene Tunney in boxing and Ty Cobb in baseball. Everything being equal, I always said those two guys would beat you because they were ahead of the game in their sports, intelligence-wise.

It is so important to have that factor of intelligence, so that you know the pitcher, know what he does, how he gets you out, what he's capable of, you know the situation of the game, you know what you did the time before, the series before. Everything works into that particular day — the wind, the elements, everything — even the catcher maybe. A guy like Cobb would have studied each catcher's style — the different way each one called his game — and could readily adjust his hitting strategy to a change of catchers. And not only was Cobb intelligent, he was also talented and completely fearless — a deadly triple threat.

On three different occasions Cobb and I got together and talked nothing but baseball. I never really did read a book on Cobb's hitting theories, but I talked to him, and there were some things that Cobb said that I personally, from my own experience, could not agree with. For example, he said when a ball was outside he stepped a little more outside, and when the ball was inside he stepped away. You can't do that! You have to plant your feet while that ball is on its way, and you can't tell whether it's inside or outside, or whether it's outside and going to break inside, or inside and going to break outside. So you have to have a happy medium all the time — and you control all that with your hands. If it's inside, you keep your hands in. If it's outside, you might have to push it out.

He held his hands three to five inches apart on the bat, and I sure couldn't hit that way, but it was probably quite conducive to his hitting .400. Sure, he probably thought he was the best ever, but why shouldn't he? He dominated everyone else during his era. He used to tell me, "Boy, Ted, if they'd pulled that shift stuff on me I'd have shown them something." He was always after me to go to left field more.

Cobb was a smart guy, and I liked him. The guy who wrote that I had a falling-out with him is full of it. We were good friends, and remained on good terms right up until the time of his death. We got along very well, and he was always very nice to me.

As I've said, he was the smartest guy I ever met in baseball, along with Hank Greenberg. But they say that on the field he was a genuine son of a bitch. (I'm just going by what they say.) Former Red Sox owner Tom Yawkey's uncle owned part of the Detroit Tigers, and he got to know Cobb and he respected Cobb so much, but when they went on a hunting trip and had a fight it broke up a friendship.

I do know that Hall of Famer Eddie Collins, who as a member of the Philadelphia A's and the Chicago White Sox played against Cobb for 22 years, revered him as a player. Eddie used to sit in the Red Sox dugout and regale us with wonderful stories about Cobb's antics. Tyrus Raymond Cobb and Babe Ruth were the two players that Collins idolized. Collins was from the old school — the Cobb era — but he had seen Babe Ruth's complete career, the whole record, and of course he realized how important Ruth had been to the game. But he also knew how important Cobb had been to the game. He had that unique perspective on the two giants of baseball.

It's no accident that Ty Cobb was the first player inducted into the Hall of Fame when it opened its doors in 1939. There's a memorable picture of three other original inductees — Ruth, Honus Wagner, and Walter Johnson — sharing the glory of the moment with various baseball notables, and it's ironic that Cobb is absent from this vanguard of American baseball heroes. It's too bad, because for many people the image that *does* endure is the picture of Cobb sliding into second base with his spikes sharpened and poised to maim. He represented a win-at-all-cost fanaticism that I guess our society grudgingly admires but ultimately rejects. Accurate or not, that's what people associate him with. But Cobb was the guy! You've got to put Tyrus Raymond in this book because, hell, nobody else ever did what he did.

A baseball old-timer was once asked by a fresh young sportswriter how the immortal Georgia Peach, Ty Cobb, might fare in today's "new and improved" game. "Oh, he'd probably hit about .320 or so," allowed the old man. "Is that all?" shrugged the reporter. "That's not so great." "Maybe not," came the reply, "but you've got to remember that Cobb would be 105 years old."

BALLPARK FIGURES: Cobb's historic hitting feats were showcased in Detroit's Bennett Park, later to become Navin Field (now Tiger Stadium). While precise dimensions from his early career are sketchy, left field measured 345' in 1921, and centerfield fences were 467' away in 1927. Right-field barriers stood some 370' from home plate in 1921.

7 Stan Musial

++

Career: 1941–1963

Bats: L   **Height: 6'**   **Weight: 175**

++

In St. Louis they erected a statue of Stan Musial frozen in that trademark stance of his: coiled and ready to hit. The inscription on the base reads, "Here stands baseball's perfect warrior. Here stands baseball's perfect knight." Well, he may not have been perfect, but he was pretty darn close. The way Stan stood at the plate, the distinctive way he wore his Cardinals cap, his easy manner when he signed autographs for kids — the way he conducted his baseball life — they all suggested a man who had escaped from a Norman Rockwell cover on the Saturday Evening Post. He wasn't glamorous like DiMaggio, or controversial like me. He had the image of a wholesome hero who represented the way things darn well ought to be in America. He was Andy of Mayberry with a bat, and everyone loved him.

Even though his stance might have been different, I have this feeling that Musial might have been a Joe Jackson type of hitter, because I know Jackson hit a lot of balls to left center and right center, and he hit a ton of triples. Musial was a slashing, all-around-the-ballpark hitter but he also hit to left center and certainly to right center quite a bit. That's where he could pull the ball more. And there's a guy who definitely *learned* how to pull the ball. When he first came up he was hitting like he had two strikes all the time, and then he got to where he was taking a pitch and waiting for a certain pitch, and finally he reached the point where he was a lot more selective. Then he got a ball he could do something with. They didn't know how to

Stan Musial: the kind of hitter — and the kind of man — for whom they erect statues. AP/WIDE WORLD PHOTOS pitch him, so they'd try him inside and he'd rip the ball to right. I'm just making an educated guess when I make that comparison with Jackson. It's a theory of mine.

Just look at Musial's record. He was the best hitter in the National League for almost 20 years. The son of a gun was a .331 lifetime hitter and captured seven batting titles in the process. He also hit 475 career homers. Who says power and average don't mix? He led the National League in total bases six times and amassed 300 total bases or more 13 times. He outslugged the rest of the senior circuit on half a dozen occasions. He was as durable as he was talented, too. He played in a hundred or more games for 21 consecutive seasons — 3026 games in all. Until Aaron and Pete Rose finally surpassed him, he held most NL batting records, including most at-bats (10,972), runs scored (1949), base hits (3630), and RBIs (1951). He batted over .300 17 times, and drove in a hundred or more runs ten times. In all, he appeared in 24 All-Star games.

Musial could run — I mean he could *run* — which helped his hitting, but I've seen him hit all types of pitching. Every time I watched him play, he really roped them. He once hit five home runs in a doubleheader.

My son John Henry came up to me at a baseball function one time and I said, "There's Stan Musial over there, John Henry. There's one hell of a hitter!" Well, you know, he thinks that his dad is the greatest hitter who ever lived. He's convinced of that. So he said, "Do you really think he was as good a hitter as you were?" I said, "Yeah, I really think he was."

When I was at the 1960 World Series, a woman came up to me, told me I was her favorite ballplayer, and asked for my autograph. While I was signing, she casually mentioned that she was Stan Musial's mother. I told her she should be giving me *her* autograph.

Now Musial was a little bit different from me. I had a little more power than Stan did. If I could have run like Musial, I don't think there would have been that much comparing — but Stan Musial could *run*.

I played against Musial in 15 All-Star games and I played against him in one World Series, in 1946, where neither of us did very well at the plate. I've seen him play a lot of times, and even when I wasn't playing against him he was always on the newsreels. So I know that Musial was absolutely something extra. That speed of his helped him tremendously.

As a hitter Musial was a sweeper and an inside-outer and a ripper to right field. He actually had a pretty big swing, but the fact that he hit the ball to center and left center a lot actually shortened the swing enough so that he couldn't be jammed, because he was so far away from the plate anyway. The farther you hit the ball through center and left center to the opposite field to which you would pull the ball, the farther back you are when you hit the ball. So it was a little harder for Musial to pull the ball for a while. But then he got to the point where he knew that little game between the pitcher and the hitter, and he started to take full advantage of that knowledge.

He was a better all-round hitter than Hank Aaron. He won his final batting title at the age of 36, when he hit .351. And he was still among the league leaders when he was 41, hitting .330 in 1962, his next to last year. He was a hell of a hitter, and a fine all-round ballplayer. He was a quiet leader on the field and in the clubhouse and was one of the most universally respected ballplayers of our generation. He wasn't the biggest guy in the world, but he was a lithe 6'1", 175 lbs, and he was whippy. When he made his exit from baseball he did it with a pair of solid base hits — very little flamboyance but an abundance of style. The kind of hitter — and the kind of man — for whom they erect statues.

For a left-handed hitter, Stan Musial handled southpaw pitchers very well. Even Hall of Famer Warren Spahn, who recorded more wins (363) than any other leftie in major league history, was mere batting practice for Stan the Man. Musial batted .314 lifetime, with 14 homers against Spahn. "He's the only batter I ever intentionally walked with the bases loaded," Spahn once admitted.

BALLPARK FIGURES: Sportsman's Park was Stan Musial's hitting ground throughout his spectacular career. The left-handed hitter faced the following dimensions: left field — 351.1'; left center — 379'; centerfield — 420'; right center — 354'; right field — 309.5.

8 Shoeless Joe Jackson

Career: 1908–1920

Bats: L　　　　**Height: 6'1"**　　**Weight: 200**

o me it's ironic that in the Baseball Hall of Fame in Cooperstown, N.Y., the place dedicated to honoring the greatest players of the most American of all sports, there is no plaque bearing the name and likeness of Joe Jackson. No statue of Shoeless Joe. None of the bats that he once used to wreak havoc on the American League. Lord knows it's not because he wasn't good enough to be included in those hallowed halls, because his feats certainly surpass those of many of the players enshrined there. Jackson was absent only because he was *accused* of conspiring to fix the 1919 World Series and was banned from baseball.

Even though Jackson didn't have a long career, every record, every evidence, every comparison, everything pertaining to our selection formula gives him a high ranking. Even though he played in the dead ball era, you're still compelled to put him up there, with his high production numbers. Ty Cobb earned his place on the list with his .367 batting average and his complete domination of the league, but Jackson wasn't far behind with a .356 average and the sweetest swing imaginable. For me Jackson's hitting style was vastly superior to Cobb's. Jackson was my kind of hitter.

Using a bat he called Black Betsy, Shoeless Joe established the third-highest batting average in baseball history. Only Cobb and Hornsby (.358) were higher. In 1911, his first full major league season, Jackson hit .408 — and *still* he didn't win the batting title,

Shoeless Joe Jackson: there never was a better pure hitter. NATIONAL BASEBALL LIBRARY & ARCHIVE, COOPERSTOWN, N.Y.

because Cobb picked that year to hit .420! The next season Jackson batted .395 and Cobb responded with .410. Same thing in 1914, when Jackson hit .373 and Cobb .390. He was always playing in Cobb's shadow, and yet there is still no doubt in my mind as to who was the better pure hitter. With all of that statistical evidence going for him, I had to put him in this book, and I did so knowing that in the eyes of baseball he was barred as being unworthy. He was never actually convicted, but in the eyes of baseball he was guilty. I know his selection will create controversy because a lot of baseball people still feel that way. So be it. There's nothing controversial about Joe Jackson except that he was thrown out of baseball. His record is perfectly legitimate.

I didn't base my decision solely on statistical evidence. Every hitter who ever saw Joe Jackson, every player who ever saw Joe Jackson, said that he was in a class by himself. Players who played with him and against him agree on that. There was never a single one I spoke to who didn't say, "Well, he was probably the greatest hitter who ever lived." In the older days, up to 1919 or 1920, he was revered as a hitter more than Cobb was. Cobb was revered as a tough, daring, spirited, all-out, gung-ho ballplayer, and you certainly have to admire that. But Jackson — just for hitting the ball and looking good doing it — was considered the greatest. He was a classic hitter.

Personally I can't conceive of anyone looking as good with their hands three to five inches apart — like Cobb — as a guy with his hands down toward the end of the bat swinging fluidly. And that's the kind of hitter Jackson was.

I'm on the veteran selection committee for the Hall of Fame, and I brought Shoeless Joe's name up in the old-timers' meetings just to feel the committee out. Boy, there was a hell of a storm, and I could soon see they wouldn't tolerate that. God, I really got shouted down for bringing his name up for consideration. One guy especially objected. He said, "I looked it all over, Ted, and you can forget about him!"

Well, all the books are supportive of Jackson. All the records say that he tried to give the money back. He still led everybody in batting in the 1919 World Series. He hit .365 and had a good Series and all the rest of it. If he was trying to throw the Series, he did a damn poor job of it. Nevertheless, he was banned forever from the game he was born to play.

Apparently, away from the baseball diamond Jackson wasn't a very smart guy. A great hitter, but not very smart. Baseballic intelligence and street smarts are two different things. I've seen otherwise intelligent guys who could swing the bat and were pretty good hitters, and you wonder why they weren't better, and invariably it's because they were so damn dumb about what's going on at the plate. Baseballically Joe Jackson was smart. Unfortunately he wasn't very smart about a lot of other things in life.

It was a crying shame, because everybody who saw him, including Eddie Collins, who was on that Black Sox team with Jackson in 1918, said he was the best. Collins was later an executive with the Red Sox — a man who spent 60 years of his life in baseball, a Hall of Famer who has a lifetime .330 average. Collins always compared me with Shoeless Joe, and that was such a great compliment. He said, "Ted, you're the closest thing I saw to Joe Jackson," and, "All I could think about when I saw Ted Williams was Joe Jackson." That's pretty heady stuff for a young hitter. Even today it remains one of the highest compliments I've ever received in the game of baseball: having my swing compared with Shoeless Joe's.

And Babe Ruth said he *copied* Joe Jackson — so you know Joe was a great hitter. Ruth was proud to have modeled his swing on Shoeless Joe's.

Obviously I never saw Shoeless Joe hit, but Collins saw that resemblance between us right away. He first saw me as a young rookie in San Diego, and I wasn't even playing at the time. I was just taking batting practice, and Collins went to the owner and asked who that kid — that left-handed hitting kid — was. "Oh, he's only a youngster who's just out of high school," Collins was told. "He's three or four years away." And still Collins said at the time, "Just give me first chance at him." And I wasn't even playing! He was really out there looking at Bobby Doerr and Georgie Myatt. That proves that Eddie Collins was as astute an observer of baseball and batters as anyone who ever lived. Not only was he a shrewd judge of opposing players, but he had that uncanny ability to assess potential in young hitters. Right away he saw something that no one else saw. He told old Bill Lane, "Just give me an option on him." And the very next year they picked me up and I went to the Red Sox. So even though I didn't see Shoeless Joe Jackson hit, Eddie Collins saw him and played alongside him, and that's good enough for me.

From anything I can ever find and read and research about Joe Jackson and his ability to hit, he stood head and shoulders above the rest. The great hitters of his day all sang his praises. He had the admiration of every player and fan until the scandal broke.

He was never around at any of the old-timers' functions, and I still regret that I never met him. For six or eight years during the '40s the Red Sox used to go through Charleston, South Carolina, on our way to spring training, and that little town of Charleston was where Jackson lived out his remaining years. I don't know yet why Cronin didn't say to me, "Why don't you go over and see Joe Jackson and say hello to him?" Ted Williams and Joe Jackson! That would have been one hell of an interesting conversation on hitting.

But even then, more than 25 years after the scandal first broke, Jackson was a real outcast from baseball. The game turned its back on him and he was blackballed. The old-timers all knew what he had done, but he was dropped so fast and so completely from baseball that until Hollywood rediscovered him recently, most people just forgot about him. And it's too bad, because he was so damn great.

Sure he made some bad mistakes, mostly because he wasn't too smart . . . but it's too bad.

Generations of fans have made the pilgrimage to Cooperstown and returned home with the mistaken impression that they have seen all the great hitters who played this game. Well, that's not quite true. That's why I'm proud to include Joe Jackson on my list of the greatest hitters of all time. On my personal field of dreams, he'd be right there in the batter's box where he belongs.

In the early days of baseball, bench jockeying was an accepted weapon for distracting opposing hitters, and some of the barbs could be exceedingly cruel. Shoeless Joe Jackson was decidedly lacking in book learning, a fact that was not lost on rival teams. As he stood at the plate awaiting the next delivery one hot August after-noon, a leather lung in the enemy dugout bellowed, "Can you spell illiterate?" Jackson responded with a stinging line drive and ended up in a cloud of dust on third base. Brushing himself off, he turned towards his tormentor and with a devilish grin asked, "Can you spell triple?"

BALLPARK FIGURES: Shoeless Joe's original fields of dreams were League Park in Cleveland (1910–1915) and Comiskey Park in Chicago (1915–1920). League Park's dimensions were 385' to left field, 505' to deepest corner, left of center, 420' to center, and 290' to right field. Comiskey was 362' down the foul lines, 382' to the power alleys, and 420' to centerfield.

9 Hank Aaron

††††††††††††††††††††††††††††††††††††††

Career: 1954–1976

Bats: R **Height: 6'** **Weight: 190**

††††††††††††††††††††††††††††††††††††††

ank Aaron didn't have that much charisma, especially compared to Mantle and Mays. The usual knock on him is that he was too quiet, too colorless, and too predictable. But remember this: a Stealth missile is quiet too, and Clark Kent was colorless until he ducked into that phone booth. As for being predictable, Rolls Royce made its reputation by producing finely tuned, predictable cars.

Aaron wasn't one of those guys who sought the limelight, and playing in places like Milwaukee and Atlanta, he didn't get that much media attention. At least not until he began to threaten Babe Ruth's 714-homer mark. That got the writers' journalistic juices flowing, and all of a sudden they wouldn't leave him alone. But he had the courage to overcome the pressures and dethrone a white American icon in the heart of the South.

Hank Aaron was one of the truly great hitters. I used to talk with the National League pitchers and they'd either talk about Aaron or Mays. The consensus seemed to be, "I don't know how to pitch to either of those two guys. They crack everything!" Some pitchers said, "I have to brush them back," or, "I have to loosen them up," or, "I've got to try to keep them honest." God, both of those guys were wonderful hitters.

For this book I am going to refer to Aaron as the "Home Run King," because he "quietly" hit more homers than anyone else. I don't think it's fair to say he's the greatest home run hitter, but he's the Home Run King and I think he'll forever have that title. He

Aaron overcame the pressures and dethroned a white American icon in the heart of the South. NATIONAL BASEBALL LIBRARY & ARCHIVE, COOPERSTOWN, N.Y.

hit more home runs, 755, than any other player who will probably ever live, and he drove in 2297 runs while maintaining a .305 batting average over a 23-year major league career.

He sure had longevity, and coupled with the fact that he was a hell of a hitter, that made him the Home Run King. Like a lot of great hitters I know, with Aaron you make a mistake and he cashes in on it. I think Aaron was a classic mistake hitter.

For 20 consecutive years Aaron hit 20 or more home runs per season; for 15 seasons he topped the 30-homer mark, and eight times he hit 40 or more. He led or tied for the league lead in homers four times and drove in a hundred runs 11 times. In 1957 he captured the National League MVP award, hitting 44 home runs and driving in 132 while batting .322.

One day in spring training I was managing with Washington, and Joe Coleman was pitching for us in an exhibition against the Braves. I said, "Joe, listen. You're going to pitch against a great hitter today — Mr. Henry Aaron. Now, just have a little fun and try to see what you can do. The first time up give him nothing but breaking stuff, breaking stuff, breaking stuff." So first time up, on the third pitch he hit a ground ball to short. The next time Aaron was up, I told Joe, "Do the same thing: breaking ball, breaking ball, breaking ball." Well, he hit another ground ball to shortstop. Now the next time Aaron got up, I went to Coleman and I said, "Joe, the first pitch throw the hardest, fastest high fastball you can throw." He threw a blazing high fastball — and remember, Aaron hadn't seen one all day — and he hit a goddamn rocket out of left field. He just hammered it! That really showed me something. When he got a pitch to hit, he missed it less often than anybody else. Other guys fouled them off, or they'd take the pitch, but not Aaron. He drilled them.

They talked about the power of Aaron's wrists, and it's true he was a little "wristy," or he appeared that way. He was a great hitter, and he could get the ball in the air with a nice kind of level swing. He had great ability to get the ball in the air. You can hit howitzer shells through the infield and they're still singles, but those same shots in the air are the ultimate hits — home runs, or at least extra bases. So that puts a premium on guys like Henry Aaron who can get the ball in the air consistently.

I don't take one thing away from Aaron. I know how great a hitter he was. I also have the greatest respect for Henry Aaron as a super all-round player. But you can never make me believe that he was the best player of all time. I saw more of DiMaggio, and that's the reason I thought he was the greatest player I saw. Aaron and Musial and Mays were all super players, though, you can't deny that.

So what if Aaron played in a hitter's ballpark in Atlanta? You've got to have some advantages in your career in order to have a lot of good things happen. He sure did have longevity, but he hit consistently throughout his long career. The only thing that I can say about him as an intelligent hitter is that his record emphatically proclaims that he was. There may be some unintelligent guys who can still hit .340 for one season, but to have a successful career you've got to have that one important factor of being baseballically alert to what's going on with that pitcher and you, and what's gone on in the past.

Aaron made baseball history on the field, and now he's in the front office in Atlanta. He's one of those guys who's serious about where he wants to be in the annals of the game.

As a shy rookie from Mobile, Alabama, in 1954, Hank Aaron was an inviting target for bench jockeys and veteran players from opposing teams. Legend has it that he was once scolded by an opposing catcher for not holding the bat label toward him, as was the accepted custom of the day. Aaron's succinct reply spoke volumes about baseball's future Home Run King: "Didn't come up here to read, came up here to hit," mumbled Hammerin' Hank.

BALLPARK FIGURES: For most of his record-breaking career, Aaron played his home games at Milwaukee's County Stadium (1954–1965) and Atlanta's Fulton County Stadium. In Milwaukee the dimensions were 320' to left field, 355' to the short alleys, 376' to the power alleys, 397' to the deep alleys, 410' to centerfield (402' starting in 1955), and 315' to right field. Fulton County Stadium was 325' down the foul lines, until 1967 when it became 330'. Left center was 385' in '66, 375' in '69 and 385' in '74. Centerfield was 402' in '66, 400' in '69, and 402' in '73. Right center was 385' in '66, 375' in '69, and 385' in '73.

10 Willie Mays

++++++++++++++++++++++++++++++++++
Career: 1951–1973

Bats: R   **Height: 5'11"**   **Weight: 187**

++++++++++++++++++++++++++++++++++

illie Mays was one of the most exciting and charismatic ballplayers of his era. Because of his remarkable sense of drama, and the fact that he played in larger media centers, he often overshadowed his chief National League rival, Hank Aaron. While Aaron seemed content with being the consummate ballplayer, Mays was also the consummate performer, always drawing the spotlight. They were like two sides of the same coin. You could say that Aaron had a flair for consistency while Mays had a consistent flair.

Willie Mays was an absolutely sensational, super ballplayer. He did everything well. Despite his Hall of Fame statistics, he was one of those guys you really had to see to appreciate just how good he was. He played the game with controlled abandon. On the basepaths he was in perpetual motion: stealing bases, disrupting pitchers' concentration, stretching singles into doubles, doubles into triples. He won 11 consecutive Gold Gloves, and his patented basket catches in centerfield were imitated on every sandlot in America. In the level of excitement he generated and the sheer joy he brought to his game, Mays was the Michael Jordan of the '50s and '60s. My idea would be that if DiMaggio wasn't the best all-round player I ever saw, then Mays probably was. A lot of people say that Mays was a better hitter than Aaron, but Aaron is still the home run champion. Both are just over .300 in lifetime average, with Mays edging out Aaron .305 to .302. So it's really hard to rank those two guys.

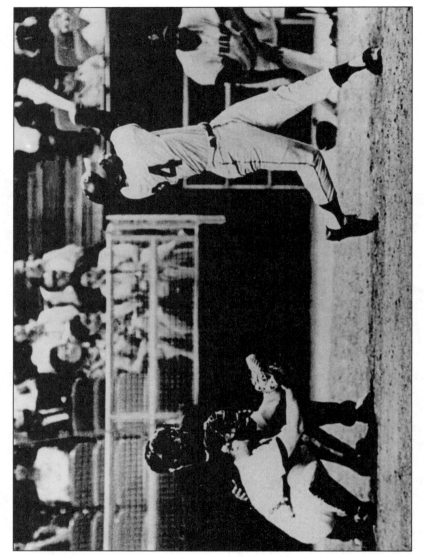

Mays was the Michael Jordan of the '50s and '60s.

My most vivid memory of Mays is that he was a big swinger. He could swing at bad balls — and he could hit bad balls, too. He was a hard swinger. Of all the wild swingers he was probably the best, because he had extreme power. If he could get ahold of a ball — no matter where the pitch was — if he could get it in the air, it was good-bye Charlie! Yes, he swung at an awful lot of bad balls; but I even feel guilty talking like that because he was so damn great.

When he first came up in 1951 he struggled, much the same way Mantle struggled when he came up with the Yankees. Leo Durocher was able to boost his confidence, just as Stengel did for Mantle, and Mays went on to help the Giants win the pennant in his rookie year.

As I look back — and I saw Mays hit in different places — he was a lot like Mantle: if he didn't hit it well he still had a hell of a chance to get a base hit, and if he hit it well it went out of sight. He had tremendous power to all fields. I used to think he had a shot at .400. He was just one of those rare types of guys. Mantle would hit a dribbler and, hell, it was a base hit; Mays hit a dribbler and it was a base hit. Mays could run faster than Aaron, but those two guys both had the talent plus.

Mays led the National League in home runs four times, in triples three times, in hits once, and in batting once. Twice he passed the magic 50 home run barrier in a season, and he once hit four in a single game. He topped the league in on base percentage twice, in slugging percentage five times, and in overall production five times. Ten times he exceeded a hundred RBIs. He was named MVP in 1954 on the strength of a league-leading .345 average and 41 homers, leading the Giants to yet another pennant in the process. He continued his dominance well into the next decade and was named Player of the Decade for the '60s by *The Sporting News.* In 1962 he led the charge to another pennant, this time in San Francisco, and in 1965 he won another MVP award with his second 50-homer outburst.

In the All-Star game he stood out like no one else, even in the midst of those other great players. He turned it into his personal showcase and he was absolutely brilliant. He took the game seriously and helped the National League to a string of wins with his agressive play.

Mays did some things that nobody else did. He was a muscular, stacked-up son of a gun, and yet he ran like a deer. He led the National League in stolen bases four times and finished with a total of 337 career steals. Willie was the first to hit 300 homers *and* steal 300 bases, pioneering that combination of power and speed that you see in today's game. I'd put Mays and Mantle in the top rank because of the devastating power both had. You're talking about over 1200 home runs between them, for God's sake.

Who would I take first on my ball club, Mantle or Mays? It would be a hell of a tough decision. You take one and I'll take the other. It's the same with DiMaggio. You can put him with that group too. For me DiMaggio was a little smoother than either one of those guys, but he was not as awesome swinging a bat. Just smoother, more stylish.

The National League was ahead of the American League in getting the black players, and I've been all for that. My 1965 Hall of Fame induction speech at Cooperstown shows you how I felt about it. Once Jackie Robinson signed with the Brooklyn Dodgers, the entire National League benefited for years to come. Understandably, the great black players gravitated to the league that had broken the color barrier. It got some super players, including three Hall of Famers, in that era: Aaron, Frank Robinson and Willie Mays.

I still can't believe that Mays and Mantle barely hit .300. They are both just on the brink (Mantle just missed with .298). That's hard to believe, especially with that speed plus that both of them had. Both were free-swinging guys, two of the greatest that God ever allowed to play this game.

Willie Mays hit for power and average and roamed the outfield with the speed and grace of a gazelle. One of the most fitting compliments that he was ever paid was accorded by Bob Stevens, following a game-winning triple in the 1954 All-Star game. Wrote Stevens, "The only man who could have caught it, hit it."

BALLPARK FIGURES: Mays played out of New York's Polo Grounds (1951–1957) and Candlestick Park in San Francisco (1958–1972). The Polo Grounds' dimensions were 279'–280' to left field, 447' to left center, 480'–483' to center, 449' to right center, and 257' to right field during his stay there. Windy Candlestick Park was 330'–335' to left field during Mays' time there. Left center was 397' in 1960 and 365' starting in 1961. Centerfield was 420' in 1960 and 410' in 1961. Right center was 397' in 1960 and 375' in 1961. Right field was 330' in 1960 and 335' in 1968.

11 Hank Greenberg

†††††††††††††††††††††††††††††††††††††

Career: 1930–1947

Bats: R   **Height: 6'3½"**   **Weight: 215**

†††††††††††††††††††††††††††††††††††††

Hank Greenberg destroyed the popular image of power hitters as lumbering behemoths with more brawn than brains. He was one of the most intelligent guys I ever met in baseball, and his record supports my theory that intelligence is a key ingredient in becoming a great hitter.

If Hank Greenberg could have run, he would have hit 15 points higher — and he was a .300 hitter anyway. He lost some very good years to the Second World War too, but if he'd had speed he really could have added to his record.

That's just another ingredient that helps a hitter. That's another thing about Ruth: he couldn't run that well either, but he was still a .342 hitter and he hit all those home runs. It's scary to think he could have been even more devastating with speed. Same thing with Greenberg. You can't deny that it would have added to their legend.

During an abbreviated career than spanned parts of 13 seasons with Detroit and Pittsburgh, Greenberg stroked 331 home runs while maintaining a .318 batting average. The towering 6'3½", 215-lb first baseman captured five American League home run titles, batted .300 nine times, and led the league in RBIs on four separate occasions, including a 183-RBI outburst in 1937. He hit a dramatic grand slam against the St. Louis Browns to clinch the 1945 pennant for the Tigers on the last day of the season. In all, he led the Tigers to four American League pennants and hit well

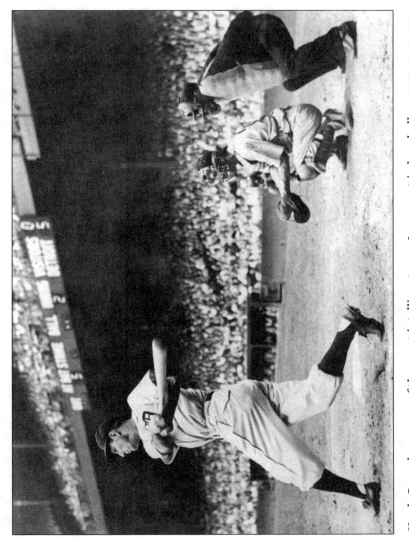

Hank Greenberg: one of the most intelligent guys I ever met in baseball. NATIONAL BASE-
BALL LIBRARY & ARCHIVE, COOPERSTOWN, N.Y.

over .300 in World Series play. When he was later traded to Pittsburgh, he was instrumental in helping Ralph Kiner hone his Hall of Fame hitting skills.

Of all the big hitters that I talked to, I probably talked more with Greenberg alone than with any other hitter, but the funny part of it was, his questions weren't about how you swung or how you hit a high ball or a low ball or anything like that. He was a great hitter himself and he didn't need to know that. No, he wanted to talk about every pitcher in the league, and he was always asking, "How'd that pitcher pitch to you?" I'm sure he wasn't worried about telling the Tigers what I was telling him, but he wanted to hear what I had to say.

He was always rated as a smart hitter. Pitchers knew that you didn't give him too much of the same thing, because he'd lay for it and he'd hit it. Probably the only ball that he couldn't defend against *all* the time was that extra-good high fastball. They thought they could pitch him high and tight. I know that. The pitchers all wanted to throw him their best fastball. And you know, I think even DiMaggio would say, "Show me a guy who can really buzz that high fastball and he's going to be kind of tough." But a high fastball to Greenberg — as good as he was — and a high fastball to DiMaggio were two different things. With Joe you'd better get it within an eight- or ten-inch circle or he'd nail you. His area of vulnerability was smaller than Greenberg's.

But as I've said, Greenberg was very smart. He'd usually take that pitch for a ball, or the pitcher would make a mistake and he'd get a base hit. And he'd hang in there, and next time up they'd make another mistake and he'd hit the long ball. I thought Feller was the greatest pitcher of my time, and I really think Greenberg thought so too. He'd say, "Jeez, that son of a gun is something else, isn't he?" That was the nature of my conversations with him. He spoke in general terms and didn't divulge too much. I thought Greenberg was a great guy.

My most vivid memory of Greenberg was that he'd hit a ball to the outfield and you'd think that you had it, and it would go back, back, back into the upper deck. A lot of times Greenberg would hit a fly ball to me in Detroit and my first reaction was, "Oh, I'll get that," and damn it, it goes deep into the seats. He didn't look like he'd smacked it that hard. It just had that little undercarry like Foxx,

Hank Sauer, Wally Post, and Wally Berger could give — Pat Seerey and Killebrew had it too. But Greenberg had the loftiest ball in the majors. Yes, he was a great hitter!

Hank's got 331 lifetime homers, but there's no question he would have hit 500 home runs, because he missed some of his best years and only managed 5193 at-bats. He was one of the first players in the American League to be drafted in 1942, so he missed pretty near four full years! And then he came back and led the Tigers' charge to the 1945 American League flag. I was a young player when he went to war. Those were big years for him to miss, because when he came back he didn't quite have it and he was on his way down then. His last two or three years were not quite up to his standards, despite the homers.

Greenberg's intelligence was a key to his success. That comes under the last category that a successful hitter needs: courage, eyesight, power, timing, and intelligence. It's more than being a guess hitter. It's proper thinking. I sure think that today's hitters are lacking in that last category: intelligence. They're lacking mostly in that last one. I can sit there in a game as a spectator and start talking to you about the players and the count, and yet the batter, who should be most aware of the situation, gets the count right to hit and he fouls the pitch off or he's late. He misses! What's to blame?

I know that I'm not smart, but the thing that made it possible for me to improve was that I did so much hitting that through trial and error I learned. I realized that when I fouled it off I've got to be quicker. I realized what I'd done wrong on a swing — whether I'd gotten too big with a swing, for example, that type of thing. That's why Greenberg was a hell of a player: smart, calculating, a guess hitter who was always a step ahead of the pitcher.

Greenberg hit a ton, but he was only a lifetime .313 hitter, and he missed out because of the war. But he still hit 331 homers. He could crush the ball. Only his limited number of at-bats kept him from a higher position on my Hit List.

In 1938 Hank Greenberg came within two home runs of matching Babe Ruth's record 60-homer performance of 1927. With two games left in the season, Greenberg's quest fizzled in Cleveland's cavernous League Park, where the left-field fence was 375 feet from home plate. As if this weren't enough of a challenge for the big right-hander, on the final day of the season Greenberg had the misfortune of facing his nemesis Bob Feller, who proceeded to fan a record 18 Tigers.

BALLPARK FIGURES: Greenberg, a right-handed power hitter, played virtually his entire career in Navin Field/Briggs Stadium in Detroit. Left field fluctuated between 367' and 340' during Greenberg's playing days. Left center was 365' in 1942, and centerfield varied between 464' and 440'. Right center was 370' in 1942, and right field shrank from 367' to 325'.

12 Mickey Mantle

†††

Career: 1951–1968

Bats: L & R   **Height: 6'**   **Weight: 201**

††

ickey Mantle was the very prototype of popularity. He had those blond good looks, that infectious grin, and a kind of farm-bred humility that melted the hearts of even the most cynical New Yorkers. It was ironic because he came out of Commerce, Oklahoma, as a shy kid, and yet he put his mark on one of the world's most sophisticated cities. The big city didn't change him that much. His popularity went well beyond the Big Apple, though. He transformed even the most ardent Yankee-haters across the length and breadth of the country. For 18 glorious summers it was almost like Mickey was the poster boy for baseball — if not for America. Every time you looked up you saw his face on one magazine cover or another. Even today his name is gold.

When he broke into the majors, I wasn't all that impressed with Mr. Mantle. That came a little later. In his rookie year, *everyone* was talking about this young Mickey Mantle. Well, I saw Mantle break in and I saw what Mickey did — or failed to do — in lots and lots of games. Now I always thought that I could appraise hitters, and I thought that I knew a lot about what a guy was going to do even after seeing him a few times. Others envied the way Mantle could swing, but I talked about the way he missed. And he did miss, and I came close to saying — and I did say it in my own mind — "I'm not sure this guy is going to make enough contact to make it in the majors." But

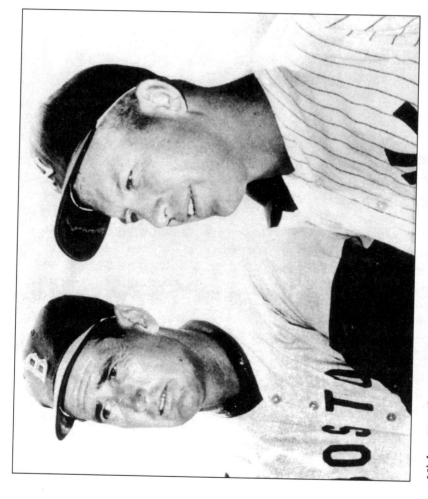

Mickey Mantle was the very prototype of popularity. BETTMANN ARCHIVE then Mantle started to make a little more contact, and then he started to really bust them, and all of a sudden he was on his way.

Now Casey Stengel was his manager at that time, and Casey was smart. He took Mickey out of the lineup before he broke *all* records for strikeouts. A rookie needs to be protected like that. When he returned to the lineup he started to make solid contact and started to hit them where few people have ever hit them. And all of a sudden he made baseball history.

Mantle was power personified. If you had to fault a great hitter like Mantle it was that he wouldn't concede a thing with two strikes. You've *got* to concede with two strikes. It's hard for me to conceive of Mickey Mantle barely being a .300 hitter. And also Mr. Mays! Two of the greatest God ever let play this game and they're barely in the .300 range. They both possessed tremendous speed, tremendous power, but they were both free-swinging guys who missed the ball an awful lot. It's really not taking too much away from them, but they absolutely should have been better hitters for average.

Mickey hardly knew what protecting the plate was. He didn't know what conceding to the pitcher meant. He didn't know that you had to hit certain pitchers a little differently than you did certain other pitchers. And *despite* all that, he was one of the greatest sluggers in baseball history.

That's the biggest difference between Mantle and Mays and Joe DiMaggio. Mantle and Mays didn't concede much with two strikes, but you take a great hitter like DiMaggio; he conceded — even though he might come up a little bit on the bat — but he would try not to pull the ball quite so much. Mays and Mantle didn't seem too concerned with that kind of strategy. They continued to swing for the fences regardless of the count.

Mantle once told a sportswriter about a discussion he'd had with me. We had been talking about hitting, and Mickey said, "Honestly, when I got through talking with Ted I didn't know what the hell he was talking about." I had to laugh. He was a little different type of hitter. He was always swinging from the heels. He was strong and he was quick. Jimmie Foxx was pretty near the same type of hitter as Mickey, but Mickey wasn't nearly as smart a hitter as Jimmie was. Jimmie was pretty damn smart. He had a baseball mind. He knew every pitcher and how they'd pitch to him, and even though he'd strike out as much as anybody, he had a good idea what the pitcher was trying to do to him. He hit them a ton just like Mick, but he was a more consistent, more disciplined hitter.

Now I'm not saying that Mickey didn't improve and adjust. It's a matter of degree. When you're up 8000 times you mature and you learn some things at the plate, mostly through the process of trial and error. He was a great change-of-speed hitter, and after a while he knew he wasn't going to get those pitches too much anymore. So he adjusted. And after a while he knew where they were going to pitch to him. Then he got his strike zone down and consolidated a little bit, and all of a sudden he was the most feared hitter in baseball.

Mantle possessed that rare combination of power and speed. They called him the Commerce Comet. He was once timed at 3.1 seconds to first base, and that resulted in countless leg hits. He hit .365 in 1957, and that year he had something like 49 infield hits. Mickey bunted with two strikes a lot that year so he wouldn't strike out, and we on the Red Sox were thankful to God that he'd do that. He'd get a hit every time; he probably could have hit .500 that way, because he was on his way to first with everyone playing back and so he had a hell of a chance.

Mantle said recently that if they'd been talking about 40/40 (40 home runs and 40 stolen bases in the same year) when he played, then hell, he'd have done 40/40. But at that time they didn't talk about that statistic. Now they have statistics on everything. They keep statistics on the last eight games you played, for Pete's sake. "He's only hitting .262," they say, "but he's hitting .466 in his last eight games." It's gotten ridiculous.

Mantle had tremendous power and he drove in a truckload of runs. That's why the most natural comparison was with Foxx. Mantle and Foxx were both built the same and I've got to feel that they both generated great bat speed. Mickey was the only other hitter I saw who made the bat-on-ball sound that Jimmie Foxx made when he hit it. It was so distinctive that a blind man could pick out a Foxx or Mantle home run.

Mantle was the greatest switch-hitter this game will ever see. I'm talking about combining power with average. It was a skill his father taught him and he worked damn hard to master it. He hit them as far as anybody *either way*. In my opinion he was a better pure hitter right-handed even though he usually batted left. He was a legitimate home run threat from both sides of the plate, hitting 373 of his 536 lifetime homers left-handed and 163 from the right side. In 1956, when he won his first Triple Crown, he had 357 at-bats from the left side and 176 from the right. He had 39 homers, 99 RBIs, and a .342 average left-handed and 13 homers, 31 RBIs, and a .375 average right-handed (overall record: 52 HR; 130 RBI; .353 AVG.). That's a pretty good balance.

On ten different occasions Mantle hit home runs from both sides of the plate during the same game. He pretty well inspired the term "tape-measure home run" through his prodigious clouts. He once came within a whisker of hitting a ball clean out of Yankee Stadium, launching a 600-foot rocket off Pedro Ramos of the Washington Senators. But regardless of the distance, he never showed the pitcher up by standing at home plate to admire his "dinger" like they do today; he ran out each homer with his head down.

What talent he had! And he's a hell of a humble guy, with all that he did. He captured the Triple Crown in 1956 with 52 home runs, 130 RBIs, and a great .353 average, the first of two times he would go over the 50-homer mark. He won three MVP awards and led the American League in homers four times, in slugging four times, and in walks five times. Ten times he batted over .300.

One of the great records anyone will ever have and one that will never be beaten is his 18 home runs in the World Series. In the first place, no one is going to get into the World Series as often as those guys on the Yankees did. Never. He played in 12 of them, and also holds the Series records for most RBIs (40) and runs scored (42).

In 1961 Roger Maris was batting third, ahead of Mantle, and that gave Roger a big advantage in his quest to break the 60-homer mark. With Mickey waiting in the on-deck circle, there's little wonder that Roger wasn't accorded a single intentional walk that entire season. After all, Mantle hit .317, stroked 54 homers, and drove in 128 runs that year. The pitchers were forced to pitch to Maris and he saw some good offerings. Now you might argue that with Maris' 61 homers that year, Mantle was up a lot of times with no one on base. Well, Maris had almost a hundred other hits in 1961, and 94 walks, so he was still on base a lot for Mick to drive him in. There's still no question that it's a big advantage to hit behind a big hitter. The fourth batter has the biggest advantage in the lineup, *I* think, for runs batted in.

With all his natural gifts, the tragic flaw in Mantle's dramatic career was his proneness to injury. He underwent surgery on both knees, along with shoulder operations and numerous and well-documented leg ailments. His ankles were notoriously weak and apparently hampered his effectiveness from the left side. The fact that he often played in severe pain has only added to his legend.

Aside from these physical complaints, Mickey also had what I feel was a chronic Achilles' heel: his unwillingness to concede with two strikes and his tendency to strike out. Even so, his batting average stands at .298, just below the magic .300 mark. No list of great hitters would be complete without the name Mickey Mantle.

In my opinion Aaron was a better hitter than Mays or Mantle, and he had pretty good speed too, but not the speed of a Mays or a Mantle. For hitting the ball, I'd have to take Aaron over the other two. For power and speed I think that Mantle and Mays are right there together. Tremendous ability, all three of those guys.

Mickey Mantle was one of the game's premier sluggers but was prone to strikeouts. With typical self-deprecating humor, the Commerce Comet recently put his whiffs in new perspective. "You've gotta think that the average fella is gonna come up to the plate maybe 550 times during the course of a normal season," he said. "Looking at my 1710 Ks, I figure that during three of my 18 years I did absolutely nothin'."

BALLPARK FIGURES: The switch-hitting Mick played all of his home games at Yankee Stadium. Left field was 301' down the line, gradually expanding to 402', 415', and finally 457' in deepest left center. The fences were a prodigious 466' at the left of the centerfield screen, 461' in center, and 407' in right center. Right field was 295'–296'.

13 Tris Speaker

†††††††††††††††††††††††††††††††††††††††

Career: 1907–1928

Bats: L **Height: 5'11½"** **Weight: 193**

†††††††††††††††††††††††††††††††††††††††

peaker was one of the true greats of all time. They never spoke about a centerfielder in the same breath as Tris Speaker until Joe DiMaggio, and then Willie Mays, came along. Because nobody could do what Speaker could do. He had the great range in the outfield and he could hit like hell. He was the epitome of endurance, playing a hundred or more games for 19 consecutive years.

He was American League MVP in 1912 for Boston, but his best offensive performance came when he was peddled to Cleveland for $50,000 in 1916 and promptly led the AL with a .386 average and 211 hits, tying for the league lead with 41 doubles. In fact he topped the AL in two-base hits eight times and finished with a grand total of 793, an American League record. From 1909 onward he batted over .300 18 years out of 20, and he hit .350 or better nine times. The big Texan is generally acknowledged as one of the two or three best defensive centerfielders in baseball history.

Speaker was the first to play a really shallow centerfield. He always claimed that Cy Young taught him to be a great fielder. Apparently Young used to hit fungos to Speaker hour after hour after hour — until he could anticipate where the ball was going to go before he even hit it.

I'm not sure who taught him to hit, but Speaker definitely belongs on the top-20 Hit List. I'm sorry to say I never talked the specifics of hitting with him. At the time I was hitting like a son of a bitch, and

Speaker was among the aristocracy of hitters. NATIONAL BASEBALL
LIBRARY & ARCHIVE, COOPERSTOWN, N.Y.

they were trying everything to get me out, including pulling that switch on me. And Speaker gave me the greatest compliment of all the great players that I knew — not once or twice but several times. He said, "You're the greatest hitter of them all." And he played with Gehrig and Ruth and Cobb and Jackson. Other people have paid me compliments, but I admired that man so much that it meant a lot to me.

Collins revered Speaker, and Collins was my closest touch to the oldest players. He played with them and against them. He played in the dead ball era and in the lively ball era too. He didn't quit until the mid-'20s, so he's got that broad experience. He saw all the great hitters. He told me that Speaker hardly ever struck out, and when I looked it up he sure was right about that. He struck out a total of 220 times in his 22-year career. Hell, that's ten times a season. Some players do that in a week.

Speaker's career paralleled Cobb's, and as a result his hitting credits have been somewhat overshadowed, if not ignored. However, being second to Ty Cobb still places you in very select company and is sure no reason to hang your head. He hit .345 lifetime to Cobb's .367, but he hit .370 or better seven times and accumulated 3516 base hits with Boston and Cleveland. Only once did he top Cobb for the American League batting crown, hitting .386 in 1916 to Cobb's .371.

Speaker wasn't a little guy; he was a nicely built guy of about 6' and 193 lbs. He was put together pretty damn well. I do think that Tris Speaker was capable of doing a little bit more as a hitter than he did, because he played almost ten years in the lively ball era and still didn't hit as many home runs as he should have. Apparently he was a line drive type hitter, and his record number of doubles would indicate that. He also hit 223 triples, which is good for eighth on the all-time list. He held his bat low and protected the plate. Home runs were not a big priority for him, I guess, but he used his great speed to steal 433 bases in his career.

Personally I think it was just the idea that average — except in the case of Ruth and Foxx and Gehrig and a few others — was the main thing they strove for. Still, you can't deny the fact that there must have been more good hitters in those days. These guys kept the high averages over an entire career. George Brett did it one year, another guy did it one year, but the guys on my Hit List kept doing it over an entire career.

The other interesting thing about Tris Speaker is that he was a natural right-hander but had to bat and throw left because of a broken arm he got after being thrown from a horse as a teenager back in Texas. Despite the injury, he started out his career as a pitcher before finally settling in centerfield.

Speaker was dubbed the Gray Eagle because of his distinctive hair color and distinguished manner. He was considered to be part of the aristocracy of baseball, and in my mind he also belongs in the aristocracy of hitters.

Despite being on opposite sides in a divisive feud between rival factions on the 1915 Red Sox, Babe Ruth later picked Tris Speaker as the centerfielder on his all-time team. Ruth called Speaker "a fifth infielder" and insisted that he had actually seen him throw runners out at first on more than one occasion. As a pitcher, Ruth had good reason to admire Speaker, and not only for his defensive skills. Ironically, the man who was later to become the most devastating hitter in the history of the game depended on the Gray Eagle for most of the Red Sox offense as well.

BALLPARK FIGURES: The Gray Eagle's home nests were at Fenway Park in Boston and League Park in Cleveland. League Park was 376' to left field. Left of centerfield measured 450', centerfield was 420', right center was 400', and right field was 290'.

14 Al Simmons

++++++++++++++++++++++++++++++++++++

Career: 1924–1944

Bats: R　　　　**Height: 6'**　　　**Weight: 210**

++++++++++++++++++++++++++++++++++++

Al Simmons had as much raw power at the plate as anyone who ever played the game. I saw enough of him when he was in uniform during his last days as a major league player and coach in Philadelphia to know that. When I looked at Simmons he reminded me of Gargantua. Of all the hitters that I saw with a bat, he looked the most menacing. Not big and heavy, just BIG! Big arms, big hands — a big, strong, burly guy. He had a bat as long as a barge pole and he'd stride up to the plate with that thing and scare you to death. I never saw him play when he was at his peak, but he sure impressed me just to look at him.

Simmons never got the publicity of a Foxx or a Gehrig or a Ruth, but of everybody I ever talked to, I don't know a man who didn't say, "Whew, Simmons is a better hitter than Foxx, except that Foxx had that flair to hit." Over the years I've also heard people say that Joe Jackson was better than Cobb, or Gehrig was better than Ruth — and many who have insisted that Simmons outranked Foxx. But the records don't indicate that. He didn't have the power of Foxx or DiMaggio. And yet Simmons was a .334 hitter and, if your team needed a base hit, he was just about as good as any right-hander who ever went up to the plate.

He didn't make the magazine covers like Foxx and other stars of his time. My own impression is that he was a big guy who wasn't too personable, whereas Foxx was extremely popular. He didn't have much of a personality — and he didn't have too

When I looked at Simmons he reminded me of Gargantua.
BETTMANN ARCHIVE

much regard for anybody. Simmons and Cobb were both critical of me for taking a pitch an inch or an inch and a half off the plate. Today when a hitter does it, he's got "great patience; no wonder he's a great hitter." Boom, boom, boom. But Simmons and Cobb were always lambasting me. Why Cobb would do that I don't know, but he was another guy who wasn't too personable. Now when they ask *me* to compare present-day hitters like Boggs and Mattingly, I say Boggs is a better hitter day in and day out, mainly *because* he's more selective at the plate. He's a pretty smart hitter. He makes the pitcher pitch. If he's fooled he doesn't fool with it. When he's got two strikes, he'll go inside-out, inside-out. He's right there all the time. I certainly don't criticize him, like Simmons did me, for being selective at the plate.

The only time I ever really talked to Al Simmons was when he said, "How much you wanna bet you don't hit .400?" This was on the eve of the last day of the season in 1941. Now when I'd go into Detroit that year, Harry Heilmann would come on out to see me and he was as friendly as hell. He'd visit with his old friend Joe Cronin and then he'd sit down with me and give me that little resumé of his. He'd say, "Don't you worry about that right-field fence. You just hit the way you *can* hit!" But when I talked to Simmons, he swaggered down through the Boston dugout and said, "How much you wanna bet you don't hit .400?" I don't think Simmons meant anything by it; he was just that type of individual. Meanwhile Heilmann was just encouraging the hell out of me.

Simmons was known as "Bucketfoot," and they claim his left foot was pointed down the line as if he wanted to take a short-cut to third base, but his stance wasn't that unorthodox, despite what's been written. He was big and rugged and he stepped out at the plate a little bit, but his rear end and hands were always right there. You can step out and, hell, still be right there, ready to hit.

He warmed up with a .308 average in his rookie year and went on to total 253 hits and a .384 average in his sophomore season; and all of a sudden his batting stance didn't look so strange. In fact I put him right up there with Musial and Mays. He certainly belongs in the first rank.

Simmons topped the American League in 1930 with a .381 mark and repeated the feat in 1931 with a .390 average. He was the AL's MVP in 1929 with a .365 average, 34 home runs and a league-leading 157 RBIs. He led the league in hits twice and fell just short of the exclusive 3000 hit club, finishing with 2927 in 20 seasons.

He was strong. I don't know why he didn't hit for a bigger career average. Four times his average was over .380. You take four of the best years from any player that ever lived and compare them with Simmons' best. That's a good project: find out if any player, other than Cobb with his .420, .410, .401, and .390, and Harry Heilmann, averaged over .380 for four years or better — and twice hit .390. How many players have ever done that? You get that one together and you'll find out that there weren't many players like that. It's a pretty elite club. They could hold their meetings in a phone booth, there were so few.

Al Simmons was as good as there ever was, but he played in Philadelphia and no one paid any attention to what he did there. He had none of Foxx's flair, and he sure didn't hit them as far. No one will ever convince me that Simmons was as good as Foxx, but, just like Frank Robinson, he was a terribly underrated player.

Aloysius Szymanki, better known to baseball fans as Al Simmons, was hardly a textbook hitter. Critics gave him the nickname "Bucketfoot" because of his awkward tendency to pull away from pitchers towards the dugout. *New York Times* sportswriter Arthur Daley referred to him as "Unquestionably . . . the worst-looking of all top hitters. His style was atrocious. . . . He should have been a sucker for an outside pitch. He wasn't. . . . Curves should have troubled him. They didn't. In fact, he was the deadliest clutch hitter on the great Athletics team."

BALLPARK FIGURES: The right-handed Simmons played most of his career (nine full seasons) at Shibe Park in Philadelphia. Left field was 334' (1922–1925), and changed to 312' in 1926 and to 334' in 1930. Left center was 387' from 1922 to '24, changing to 405' in 1925. Centerfield was 468' during Simmons' career. Right center was 393'; right field was 380' from 1921 to '25, changing to 307' in 1926 and to 331' in 1930.

Simmons also played in Chicago, Detroit, Washington, and Boston of the AL, with short stints in Boston and Cincinnati of the NL.

15 Johnny Mize

++++++++++++++++++++++++++++++++++

Career: 1936–1953

Bats: L   **Height: 6'2"**   **Weight: 215**

++++++++++++++++++++++++++++++++++

ize was one of the really outstanding hitters in base-ball history. Every place he went, he hit. He was one of only a handful of players to hit 50 homers in a sea-son, and he did it in New York at the Polo Grounds, a park that for a hitter like Mize was even harder than Sportsman's Park in St. Louis, where he spent most of his career. Then he moved over to Yankee Stadium and hit there too. Every place he played, from the time he started to play baseball till the time he quit, he was a premier hitter.

He was a truly remarkable hitter — and I thought that a long, long time ago. In the book I wrote 25 years ago, *The Science of Hitting*, I said Johnny Mize was one of the greatest hitters of all time and he deserved to be in the Hall of Fame. It took them 12 years after that for them to put him in.

Mize was a big, burly guy who nevertheless had a smooth, effortless swing. He was another of those hitters who studied his craft and had a thorough knowledge of pitchers and their repertoire. He had to find *some* edge, because he was a .312 hitter and he didn't help himself very much running. He hit as high as .364 one year, although he couldn't run a lick. Imagine that: he got no leg hits, and he still hit .300. What would he have done with speed?

Mize burst upon the major league scene with a .329 average, 19 homers, and 93 RBIs in his rookie campaign, good enough to capture the 1936 Rookie of the Year award. He was the National

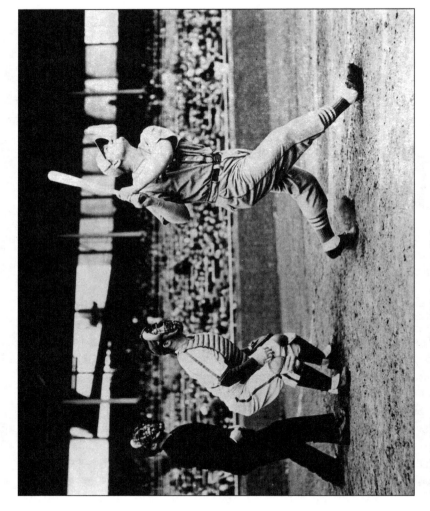

Mize hit .364 one year and couldn't run a lick. CHICAGO TODAY

League batting champion in my rookie year of 1939, with a .349 average. In total he led or tied for the league lead in homers four times, and was the RBI king three times. He went on to hit a total of 359 home runs in his 17-year major league career, but lost three prime years to the war. Although he never won the MVP award, he was in the running several times and finished second in the voting twice.

Mize hit three home runs in a game on a record six different occasions, and four times he hit three consecutive homers in one game. His greatest power binge came when he muscled a career-high 51 in 1947, a single-season record for left-handed hitters. That same year he had a slugging average of .614 and drove in 138 runs. In all, Mize captured four slugging titles, and during his career he also boasted league highs in doubles, triples, and runs scored.

His lifetime slugging percentage is .562, second to Rogers Hornsby in National League history and eighth best overall. Eight times he drove in a hundred or more runs, and he batted over .300 from his rookie campaign in 1936 until 1948. He was always among the league leaders in virtually every offensive category.

I knew from talking to him that he knew that little game that went on between pitcher and hitter. That's what helped make him a superior hitter. He talked a great deal more about hitting than DiMaggio did, for example. He really made an impact as a pinch hitter with the Yankees. I know he impressed our Red Sox club. You just held your breath when he lumbered up to bat. In a close game you really had to be worried about him, because if he didn't hit a home run, the son of a gun would draw a walk and put a guy on.

Mize was enormously strong. They called him the "Big Cat" because of smooth fielding around first base, but he also had that fluid swing that generated great bat speed and tremendous power. He could handle the best kind of fastball and the meanest curves equally well — a fine hitter who was very underrated, probably because he lost those key years to the armed services and didn't hit 500 home runs. He was a quiet guy who wasn't that popular with the press, but he was finally named to the Hall of Fame in 1980. In my opinion it was long overdue.

In the classic 1952 crosstown World Series between the New York Yankees and the Brooklyn Dodgers, Johnny Mize turned in a memorable hitting performance. He pinch-hit a homer in game three and contributed another in a game-four Yankee victory the next afternoon. He followed with a third round-tripper in as many days in an extra-inning loss in game five. Mize batted a lofty .400 in the Series.

BALLPARK FIGURES: During his peak years the left-handed Mize divided his time between two home parks: Sportsman's Park in St. Louis (1936–1941) and the Polo Grounds in New York (1942–1949). Sportsman's Park offered a 310' target in right field, 354' in right center, and 420' in center. Left center was 379' and left field was a 351' poke. The Polo Grounds' right-field fence was 257' away, right center was 440'–449', and centerfield fluctuated between 505' and 448' during his stay. Left center was 455' and left field was 280'.

16 Mel Ott

++++++++++++++++++++++++++++++++++++

Career: 1926–1947

Bats: L   **Height: 5'9"**   **Weight: 170**

++++++++++++++++++++++++++++++++++++

el Ott was the first hitter who I ever heard say, "I don't look for fastballs as much as some hitters. I look for breaking stuff." When I read that I wondered why, and he explained, "They just don't throw me many fastballs, so why would I be looking for that all the time?" That's the same theory I applied when I was looking for the slider for 15 years.

Ott's stance was a little peculiar, a little different from everyone else's, but it's results that count. He was a real slugger, and I think that of all the hitters in baseball, Ott probably best adapted himself and his style to conform to his abilities. He could pull the ball, but his greatest skill was being able to conform to the greatest advantage to the park he hit in. And that's where his detractors come in.

The biggest knock on Ott has always been that he hit 323 of his 511 home runs in that generous little bandbox known as the Polo Grounds. He used to bail out by pulling away from the first-base line, but it worked to his advantage because he was a pull hitter hitting in the Polo Grounds with that short right field porch just 257 feet away. And he crowded the plate so much that even if he did have his foot in the bucket, he still protected the plate with his bat.

Hell, he was a little guy — at 5'9", 170 lbs, the smallest guy on my Hit List — but still he was the second guy to ever hit 500 home runs, and one of only six to do it while maintaining a .300

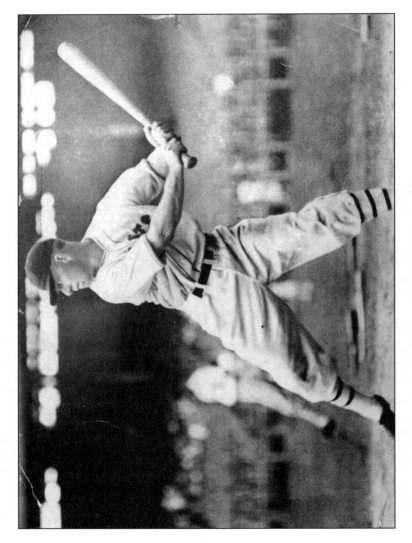

Mel Ott: no wonder they called him "the Little Giant." NATIONAL BASEBALL LIBRARY & ARCHIVE, COOPERSTOWN, N.Y.

batting average. He hit like he was ten feet tall. No wonder they called him "the Little Giant." That tells me something about his ability to adapt. He got the maximum return from his physical and mental abilities. You've got to give him a hell of a lot of credit for that, regardless of where he played.

He led or tied for the league lead in home runs on six occasions, and nine times in his 22-year career he exceeded one hundred RBIs.

A writer once asked him the obvious question: "Where did you get all that power?" His answer impressed me. "Timing, I guess you'd call it. Mostly it was a matter of connecting at exactly the right place in the swinging arc. That way I was able to get every pound behind the bat." (From *Sport Magazine*'s "All-Time All Stars," by Al Stump.) Timing. That's one of my five ingredients that make a great hitter.

Eddie Collins said that Ott used to choke up on the bat a lot for a power hitter. They said he had a little snap swing like Cobb or Wee Willie Keeler. He must have had awfully powerful wrists.

My old manager Joe Cronin had a lot of respect for Ott. Ott beat Cronin's Washington Senators with a dramatic homer off a left-handed pitcher in the opener of the 1933 World Series. And then he won the Series for the Giants with an extra-inning clout in the fifth game. He hit .389 in that Series.

Ott once hit four home runs in a single game against Philadelphia, which is a hell of a feat, but in the game that really shows what rival pitchers thought of Mel Ott, he didn't lift his bat from the shoulder once. On October 5, 1929, he was accorded five intentional walks, a league record. Now that's the kind of respect only a Babe Ruth–caliber player commands. He also holds the National League record for most bases on balls (1708) and most years with a hundred or more bases on balls (10). He was obviously patient at the plate and had a sharp hitter's eye.

Ott owned a variety of National League hitting marks until they were eventually surpassed by Mays and Aaron and others. Forty-nine times he hit two or more homers in a game. For eight consecutive seasons he powered 30 or more homers.

Referring to Ott, Leo Durocher once said, "Nice guys finish last." Leo was wrong. He finishes 16th on my list of all-time great hitters.

Chuck Klein and Mel Ott battled to the wire for the 1929 National League home run crown. Klein held a narrow 43–42 margin when his Phillies and Ott's Giants met in a season-ending doubleheader. In a flagrant display of misguided loyalty, the Phillie pitchers insured their teammate's victory by walking Ott five times, including once with the bases loaded.

BALLPARK FIGURES: The New York Giants star played his home games at the Polo Grounds. Left field varied between 279' and 280' during his career. Left center was 447' to the left of the bullpen and 455' to the right. Centerfield fluctuated wildly between 430' and 505'. Right center was 440' to 449', and right field was approximately 257'.

17 Harry Heilmann

Career: 1914–1932

Bats: R   **Height: 6'1"**   **Weight: 200**

arry Heilmann's first five years were just ordinary — and then he came on like dynamite. Cobb was the one who made him a better hitter, when he took over as manager of the Tigers in 1921. Heilmann told me personally,

When Cobb taught me how to hit inside-out, from then on I was never afraid to get two strikes on me. I could wait that much longer and still inside-out it and get the big part of the bat on the ball enough to drive it over the infielders. I didn't fear having two strikes on me after I learned that. I didn't try to pull the ball. I was aiming it through the middle, and if I had to go inside-out a little bit to get it through the middle, to get the big part of the bat on the ball — BANG — I could do it.

So he became a great hitter when Cobb taught him to go inside-out with his swing. His average just soared. That's a very important swing, and I mention it in *The Science of Hitting*. A hitter has got to learn that swing to survive, and the best way to learn it is by hitting "pepper." When you get an inside ball, keep your hands out in front of the bat and push it back through the middle. Your arms aren't completely extended like in the power swing and you don't break your wrists. You're protecting the plate. It was the answer for me

Harry Heilmann: the last American Leaguer before me to hit .400.

and it was Cobb's gift to Harry Heilmann. It's an easier way to hit, and it gives you the time to get the meat of the bat on the ball.

Heilmann's lifetime average was .342. He must have been an incredible hitter because how else could he have brought his average up to that level after five ordinary years at the start of his career? He hit under .300 his first three seasons in the majors. Then he went on an eight- or ten-year hitting spree after Cobb straightened him out in 1921. He was Cobb's star pupil, leading the league with a .394 average in his freshman year under Cobb and "graduating" with a .400 average in 1923. That's like a Ph.D. for a hitter.

Heilmann was the last American Leaguer before me to hit .400 in the majors, and I think he has the statistics to be on the Hit List. I personally never saw Heilmann hit, but I talked to Joe Cronin and Eddie Collins, who had both seen Heilmann in action. They were both impressed with him. In fact, of all the old-timers I've talked to about Heilmann, every single one has sung his praises.

He was a contemporary of Tris Speaker and Al Simmons and on two different occasions went head to head with them for the batting title in the American League. Nevertheless Heilmann is one of the least known of the great hitters to grace our top-20 group. He started slowly, but with that help from Ty Cobb he finished with a bang.

His greatest years were in the middle '20s, after he had finally learned to be a great hitter. According to Cronin he was a great line drive type hitter — on the same order as Joe Torre, the guy who used to be with the St. Louis Cardinals.

There's no question that there was a period during the '20s and '30s that produced the most gaudy hitting statistics in baseball history. Team averages and league averages soared, and records set then have never been approached since: Cobb, Sisler (twice), and Terry all had .400 seasons, while Heilmann came within a heartbeat of hitting .400 four times.

You can be cynical and disregard these hitters because of the sheer number of players with high averages. What you can't deny is the evidence. There's also no question that this was the biggest hitting era of all, which makes me believe that, generally speaking, there were better hitters in those days. Sure the ball was lively, but I don't know that the ball was any more juiced up than it is today.

There is one thing that's never talked about, though. There used to be a single seam on the ball, but in 1937 or 1938 they put a double seam on it. Now since that time there have still been guys who have hit 61 home runs, and there have been several who have hit 50, so you have to wonder whether the ball was livelier or deader as a result of the extra seam. But it's undeniable that there weren't as many good breaking-ball pitchers back in Heilmann's time, simply because — I believe — they didn't have the bigger seam to help them throw really good breaking stuff. And I think you'd find that any of the old-timers would substantiate that. They threw breaking stuff all right, just not as effectively.

Heilmann was a great hitter, but he was not a hitter in the mold of Mantle or Mays. He drove in a hundred runs eight times, but he did not excel as a home run hitter — even after the start of the lively ball era. He was still an impressive hitter, though, and once hit safely in ten consecutive trips to the plate, from June 16 to June 19, 1922.

On two different occasions Harry Heilmann battled down to the wire before capturing the American League batting title. In 1925 he refused to sit out the second game of a doubleheader to preserve his lead over Tris Speaker, and proceeded to go three for three. In 1927 the race was with Al Simmons, and again Heilmann picked up three hits in the second half of a doubleheader to win handily.

BALLPARK FIGURES: The right-handed Heilmann played most of his career at Navin Field, later to become Briggs Stadium and ultimately Tiger Stadium. Left field measured 345' in 1921 and 340.58' in 1926; centerfield was 467' in 1927; right field was 370' in 1921 and became 370.91' in 1926.

18 Frank Robinson

†††††††††††††††††††††††††††††††††††††††

Career: 1956–1976

Bats: R   **Height: 6'1"**   **Weight: 194**

†††††††††††††††††††††††††††††††††††††††

obinson is a proud and prominent name in baseball history, but when the name is mentioned most people tend to think of Jackie, who courageously pioneered the entry of blacks into the major leagues, or Brooks, who was probably the best defensive third baseman in the game's history. There's a tendency to forget about Frank Robinson, one of the top offensive ballplayers of all time. He was definitely underrated, although it's hard to see how he could have been so unappreciated based on his statistics and his accomplishments. As a fellow hitter I sure appreciated what he could do at the plate.

Frank Robinson ranks right up there in my book with Mays, Mantle, and DiMaggio. He was probably as tough a hitter in a jam as Mays or Mantle or Aaron, but they came through a few more times per time at bat. He did hit .294, though, so he's right up there with those guys. There isn't enough difference in there to make any *real* difference.

But Robinson didn't play in New York; he played in Cincinnati and Baltimore, for Pete's sake. It makes all the difference: it's easy for the big-city media to forget about players in the smaller centers.

Robinson was a great right-handed hitter who won MVPs in both the American and National leagues — and he won the Triple Crown. Who else has done all that? He was an intelligent hitter who could adapt at the plate and hit according to the situation. It's true that his ballpark in Cincinnati (Crosley Field) was a good hitter's park, but he continued to hit well after he was traded to

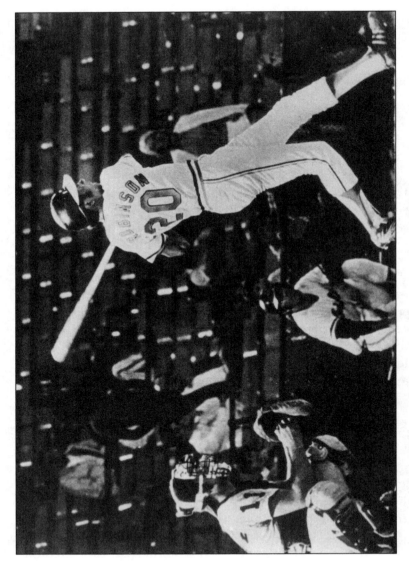

Frank Robinson: the only man to win MVP awards in both leagues. NATIONAL BASEBALL LIBRARY & ARCHIVE, COOPERSTOWN, N.Y.

Baltimore, where the ballpark had larger dimensions. The Reds traded him because they said he was "an old 30." They couldn't have been more wrong. He promptly won the Triple Crown, and in his six years with the Orioles he led them to four American League pennants and two world championships. He once hit a ball clean out of Memorial Stadium — the only player to ever do it. He had 586 home runs, while hitting just under .300 and knocking out 2943 hits. How many of today's players can make that claim?

I watched Robinson for four or five years after he'd been traded from the National League to Baltimore, and I saw just enough of him to know that he was one of the most aggressive hitters of the modern era. He played with a ferocity and a will to win that any modern-day manager would die for. And he could hit in the American League and he could hit in the National League. In his first year (1956), the big right-hander set the major league record for most homers by a rookie, with 38, and went on to win the Rookie-of-the-Year Award. When he captured the coveted Triple Crown in 1966, he hit 49 homers, drove in 122 runs, and batted .316. He led the NL in slugging percentage in '60 and '61 and topped the AL in '66.

On June 26, 1970, he drove in a record eight runs in just two consecutive at-bats — and as far as I know there's only one way to accomplish that!

And what desire he had! Writers call that an "intangible," but try to convince a battle-scarred second baseman that his hell-bent-for-leather slides are intangible. He was from the old school: intimidating, calculating, always looking for an edge. Sort of like a black Ty Cobb with home run power. He crowded the plate and openly defied the pitcher to throw inside. It's no accident that he tied the World Series record for most times hit by pitches in a game.

Factor in the important detail that he was an exceptionally smart hitter, and you know Robinson was something special. He knew how to hit according to the situation. He played mind games with the pitchers and always had them at a disadvantage because he was thinking two moves ahead — like a chess player. It's a facet of baseball that doesn't get talked about much, especially in today's game, but he was a master at it. Baseballic intelligence — Robinson had it in spades.

Frank Robinson was a winner. Aside from his impressive individual records, he led the National League Reds to a World Series in 1961 and spearheaded four Oriole drives to the American League flag. He won two World Series with the Orioles, in 1966 and 1971.

Following the tradition of his namesake Jackie, he became the first black man to manage a major league team. That event didn't get nearly the same attention as Jackie's arrival in the majors, but it was a watershed event in the evolution of the game, and they couldn't have found a more deserving person to take on the challenge. He had always been a great team leader: as a player he used to have those kangaroo courts to keep the guys loose during a pennant race. And he was a damn good manager too. He's done a very credible job in the past as a skipper because he has a good baseball mind. His name looks right at home among the trio of distinguished Robinsons, and even more at home among the greatest hitters in the game.

On June 26, 1971, Baltimore's Frank Robinson, playing with a sprained back, single-handedly destroyed the Washington Senators. Robinson hit two grand slams in two successive innings, the only player to achieve such a feat. The Orioles won the game 12–2.

BALLPARK FIGURES: Robinson, a right-handed hitter, played the bulk of his career in two ballparks, Cincinnati's Crosley Field (1956–1965) and Baltimore's Memorial Stadium (1966–1971). Crosley Field was 328' to the left-field fence, 380' to left center, 387' to centerfield, 383' to right center, and 342', expanding to 366' in '58, in right field. Symmetrical Memorial Stadium provided more challenging targets for the slugging Robinson. The power alleys were 370', expanded to 385' in 1970. The distance was 360' where the seven-foot fence met the 14-foot fence and 309' down the foul lines.

19 Mike Schmidt

++++++++++++++++++++++++++++++++

Career: 1972–1989

Bats: R   **Height: 6'2"**   **Weight: 195**

++++++++++++++++++++++++++++++++

There are those players who make it to the Hall of Fame with their glove, and there are those who make it with their bat. I guess Mike Schmidt decided not to take any chances; he excelled in all phases of the game. He was the dominant offensive player of the '70s and '80s *and* he won ten Gold Gloves for his play at third. He played 2212 games at third base, third behind only Brooks Robinson and Graig Nettles at that position. There may be some room to debate whether he was a better fielder than those guys, but there's no question he was the best-hitting third baseman in history.

As a hitter Mike Schmidt was the power and thrust of the whole National League for most of his career. Schmidt was a big, powerful guy and he dominated the league in home runs pretty much on the order of Ralph Kiner. He did it longer than Kiner did, even though in many ways he wasn't as good a hitter as Kiner was. Schmidt had the league right where he wanted it, and the pitchers didn't have a clue how to handle him. That's a great feeling.

Schmidt finished his career with 548 home runs, the seventh highest total in major league history, and 1595 RBIs. He led the National League in homers eight times, in RBIs four times, in walks four times, in on base percentage three times, in slugging five times, and in runs scored once. Nine times he drove in over a hundred runs. He bested the league in the important statistic of production (OBP + SLG.) five times in his 17-year career.

Mike Schmidt was the power and thrust of the National League.
BETTMANN ARCHIVE

Schmidt hit a couple of different ways during his career, and he was successful both ways. He hit to right center for a while, and then he changed his style and had some more great years as a pull hitter. That shows how he could adapt and how he analyzed what he was doing at the plate. He was an intelligent hitter who tried to put himself in the pitcher's shoes and think like the pitcher. He led his league in bases on balls four times.

Schmidt was National League MVP three times, one of only three players to achieve that level of dominance. His home run percentage (6.56 per 100 at-bats) is the eighth highest of all time. In 1976, at Wrigley Field in Chicago, he hit four consecutive home runs against the Cubbies and rang up 17 total bases in that ten-inning game. For an encore he homered in each of his next two games.

His best single-season home run output came in 1980, when he powered 48 and led the Phillies' charge to the National League pennant. He continued his assault in the World Series, batting at a .381 clip and chipping in two more homers.

His batting average is low — at .267 the lowest on the Hit List. He also struck out a lot more than he probably should have; almost a quarter of his trips to the plate ended up that way. But you can't deny his other statistics.

I talked to Stan Musial about Schmidt, and he agreed that Schmidt was the dominant power in his league for a long time. That's good enough for me.

Like many sluggers, Mike Schmidt was susceptible to strikeouts. He whiffed approximately once every four times up and stands third on the all-time strikeout list behind Reggie Jackson and Willie Stargell. However, he also stands eighth in home run percentage (6.56) and seventh in career home runs. Schmidt powered the Philadelphia Phillies to their first World Series championship in 96 years in 1980.

BALLPARK FIGURES: Veterans Stadium in Philadelphia was part of the regrettable trend toward symmetrical stadiums. Schmidt had to contend with 330' distances down the foul lines, 371' to the power alleys, and 408' to straightaway center.

20 Ralph Kiner

╫╫╫╫╫╫╫╫╫╫╫╫╫╫╫╫╫╫╫╫╫╫╫╫╫╫╫╫╫╫

Career: 1946–1955

Bats: R   **Height: 6'2"**   **Weight: 195**

╫╫╫╫╫╫╫╫╫╫╫╫╫╫╫╫╫╫╫╫╫╫╫╫╫╫╫╫╫╫

or ten spectacular seasons Ralph Kiner was a home run hitting machine. And even though he didn't hit 500 home runs, he did hit 369 in a hurry in that abbreviated major league stretch. He hit them like he had a bus to catch.

After impressing the Pirates brass with 14 spring training homers, he broke onto the major league scene in 1946 with a league-leading 23 homers in his rookie year, and led or tied for the National League lead in homers in each of his first seven seasons. Only once, in his final campaign, did he dip below the 20-homer mark, finishing with 18 when a bad back forced him permanently to the sidelines. His 14.10 at-bats per home run ratio is second only to Babe Ruth's 11.76. That works out to 7.09 round-trippers in every one hundred at-bats, an amazing clip.

Kiner worked hard to become a better, more consistent hitter. Despite his home run crown, he had struck out over a hundred times in his rookie year and had a batting average of only .247. He wasn't content with those numbers. He studied pitchers and their deliveries much the same as I did. He even kept charts on each pitcher, and in that regard I guess he was ahead of his time. I kept my pitching charts in my head. Kiner also practiced with team-mates for hours to improve his hitting skills. He was successful in cutting way down on his strikeouts, and he raised his batting average to a respectable level in the process. He made himself a better hitter through hard work and an intelligent approach to his craft. I respect that in a ballplayer.

Ralph Kiner was born to drive Cadillacs.

A lot of people don't think he belongs in the Hall of Fame, but I sure do because he absolutely devastated the other power hitters in the league for a long time. In fact he devastated the entire league. He made a lot of noise over there, hitting 23, 51, 40, 54, and so on . . . and he did it for seven years in a row. His 54 homers in 1949 is the second highest total in National League history.

So you're damn right I believe Kiner belongs in the Hall of Fame. His domination as the biggest slugger in the National League for seven years cannot be denied.

It's too bad he wasn't on a better ball club than the Pittsburgh Pirates, who were pretty weak at the time. He didn't get much support. They pitched around him a lot and he drew a large number of walks, over a hundred per season on six occasions.

Even with the garden that they called Kiner's Korner in left field, it was still an authentic poke for a homer, and no one could ever say the park helped him *that* much, because he hit 159 of his 369 homers on the road.

Kiner hit over .300 on three separate occasions but couldn't maintain that level. He averaged over a hundred RBIs per season and led the league in that department once. He actually inspired the sentiment that home run hitters drive Cadillacs while singles hitters have to settle for Fords. It was his power that made him the highest-paid player in the National League. He drew the fans to the ballpark and they all left after his last at-bat.

Kiner was a disciple of the great Hank Greenberg, who had come over to the Pirates from Detroit in 1947 in the twilight of his career. Greenberg honed Kiner's natural ability and helped him to become a consistent power threat. He was obviously an eager student. You'd have to be crazy not to take advantage of a great resource like Greenberg. Kiner's best year came in 1949, when he powered 54 home runs and rang up 127 RBIs, both league highs. He hit 25 of those homers on the road that year, a National League record. That shows that he could hit anywhere.

When you start adding up all his statistics, Kiner was so devastating in the run production and power categories that nobody comes ahead of him, despite the fact that he has the second lowest average on my list. If his career had been a bit longer, who knows where he'd have ended up. With all due respect to the Ford Motor Company, Ralph was born to drive Cadillacs.

After Ralph Kiner had just deposited his best curve ball in the left-field bleachers, Chicago Cubs pitcher Bob Muncrief received some unsolicited advice from manager Frankie Frisch. "Never give Kiner a curve," admonished Frisch. "Throw him nothing but fastballs." On Kiner's next plate appearance, Muncrief took the advice to heart, only to watch his first fastball land in an even more remote corner of the bleachers. When Frisch made his inevitable trip to the mound, a philosophical Muncrief indicated a somewhat tarnished silver lining. "Well, Frank, he hit yours a lot farther than he hit mine."

BALLPARK FIGURES: Kiner, a right-handed power hitter, called Pittsburgh's Forbes Field his home for most of his career. Left field was 335' away in 1947 and left center was 355'. Centerfield was 435', right center was 408', and right field was 300'. Kiner's Korner, also known as Greenberg Garden, was an area in left field placed there to enhance the home run totals of both hitters.

Extra Innings

THE HITTERS: LEFT AND RIGHT, NORTH AND SOUTH

For those who are interested in such things, 11 of my top 20 hitters were right-handers, eight batted from the left side, and one, Mickey Mantle, was a switch-hitter. Eleven played primarily in the American League and nine primarily in the National League.

The location of the home states of the top 20 supports my belief that warm weather helps to cultivate hot hitters. Seven hail from northern states and 13 from the southern U.S. Texas leads the way with three selections, while Georgia, Alabama, California, Maryland, and New York each boast two. Other states represented are Pennsylvania, South Carolina, Oklahoma, Wisconsin, Louisiana, Ohio, and New Mexico.

ARGUING SOME CLOSE CALLS

Gehrig Versus Foxx

Gehrig versus Foxx is an awfully tough matchup. There are a lot of circumstances that go into a player's record. Look at Jack Dempsey in boxing: his critics say he never fought anyone — whereas there is certainly no doubt that Joe Louis took on all comers. The same applies in basketball. Despite Wilt Chamberlain's awesome statistics, critics say Bill Russell was a better player because his Celtics won more often. But there's no doubt in my mind that Chamberlain was the most dominant basketball player of his era. In the same way it's difficult to compare Gehrig, who was a left-handed hitter, and Foxx, who batted from the right side. It's always been tougher for a right-handed hitter. The ballparks favor left-handed hitters, and the fact that there are many more great right-handed pitchers also makes it tougher for righties.

Foxx was definitely the most productive right-handed hitter I ever saw; DiMaggio would be second in that department. Foxx hit 58 homers one year — and he didn't need short porches. He hit balls out of sight. I'd hate to say that anyone was better than Jimmie Foxx, but Gehrig's statistics suggest he was.

Gehrig has a slight statistical edge over Foxx.

Hornsby Versus Cobb

Don't get me wrong, I'd love to have Cobb on my team. But in a comparison of these two great hitters, I'd have to pick Hornsby every time. He hit more home runs and he was right-handed, which, as I've said, is a disadvantage for a hitter. When it comes to a choice between power and average as criteria for a great hitter, I'll pick power every time. Throughout my career everybody told me that Rogers Hornsby was the greatest right-handed hitter of all time. He hit well in St. Louis, and then he was traded to the Giants and hit .361 there — even with the death valley that they had at the Polo Grounds.

But I'd never deny Cobb's place as the greatest competitor in baseball history. Cobb was a big guy for his time and he just terrorized the American League.

Aaron Versus Mays

Aaron was the better hitter, but Mays was equally dangerous. Mays was a great runner, with great speed; I wish I'd had his speed. And he was such an exciting competitor. All I heard about both Aaron and Mays for 15 years was "I don't know how to pitch to the son of a gun," and "Boy, can he hit this," and so on. It finally got to the point where Mays started swinging at bad balls, while Aaron was a little more controlled, but those two guys were in a league of their own. Their records say it all.

Ruth Versus Me

While comparisons with Babe Ruth are always flattering, there is certainly no doubt in my mind that Ruth was the ultimate player. He did more of everything, and you can't overstate what he meant for the game of baseball.

As far as hitting is concerned, he outslugged me .690 to .634, and while I had an edge in on base percentage, his overall production numbers are staggering, the highest ever. He also had the best home run frequency of all time. I'm quite satisfied to be considered in the same company as the Babe, DiMaggio, Gehrig, Foxx, and Musial. That's plenty good enough for me.

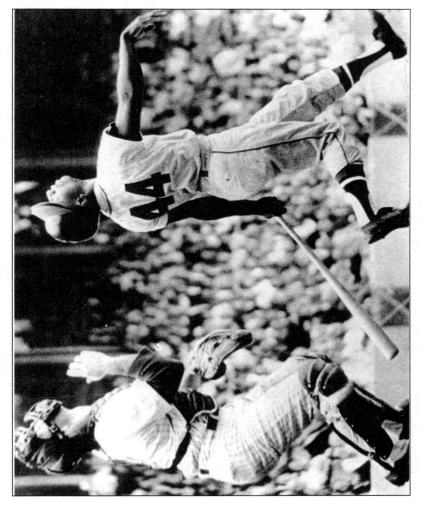

Hank Aaron: the Home Run King. LLOYD E. KLOS, ROCHESTER TIMES UNION

THE ON-DECK CIRCLE

Some Young Hitters to Keep an Eye On

Ionce had a pretty keen batting eye, and since I retired I've also done quite well in spotting potential in young hitters. Here are nine hitters who I feel have the ingredients necessary for future greatness (note: minimum of one thousand at-bats):

1 Frank Thomas — Lifetime production of .993 is the best today. Could put together Ruthian numbers. MVP.
2 Juan Gonzalez — A Killebrew, Kiner clone. Good power numbers, lower average.
3 Gary Sheffield — Challenged for Triple Crown in 1992.
4 Ken Griffey Jr. — Has all the tools for greatness: hitting, speed, instincts.
5 John Olerud — He has great attitude and a great swing.
6 Mike Piazza — I've liked his hitting from day one.
7 Carlos Baerga — A power hitter who can bat .300.
8 Travis Fryman — His numbers have been impressive.
9 Jeff Bagwell — MVP for Houston, great power.

Thoughts on John Olerud

Olerud was a lifetime .267 hitter and then all of a sudden he was pressing .400. You know, I hit .327, then .344, then — BOOM! — .406. It takes a while for everything to come together for a hitter. Olerud's in a good lineup and has the advantage of having Joe Carter hitting behind him to protect him. He's really wakened everybody up.

He reminds me more of Cecil Travis* than myself. Travis was a third baseman/shortstop for Washington from 1933 to 1947 and ended his career with a .314 average. Olerud hits more straight-away than I ever did. He gets the bat on the ball very well. He has a great attitude and always waits for a good ball to hit. But he may lack one key ingredient to make a legitimate run at .400: speed.

---

*Hall of Famer Bob Feller has included Travis, along with Williams, DiMaggio, Greenberg, Simmons, Foxx, and Charlie Gehringer, on his personal list of all-time toughest hitters. In 1941 Travis hit .359 and still missed the batting title by 47 points to a young Ted Williams. Like many other players' careers, his was dramatically and negatively affected by the Second World War. He developed frozen feet at the Battle of the Bulge and never again returned to his pre-war form. Previously he had batted over .300 in eight of his first nine seasons. As Feller indicates in *Now Pitching, Bob Feller,* despite the fact that the record books show that Travis retired in 1947 at the age of 34, "The reality is that his career was finished by the war, and his last real season was 1941, when he was 28." — Jim Prime

HALL OF FAME SPEECH, COOPERSTOWN, N.Y., JULY 1966

I guess every player thinks about going into the Hall of Fame. Now that the moment has come for me I find it is difficult to say what is really in my heart. But I know it is the greatest thrill of my life. I received 280-odd votes from the writers. I know I didn't have 280-odd close friends among the writers. I know they voted for me because they felt in their minds and some in their hearts that I rated it, and I want to say to them: Thank you from the bottom of my heart.

Today I am thinking about a lot of things. I am thinking of my playground director in San Diego, Rodney Luscomb, and my high school coach, Wos Caldwell, and my managers, who had such patience with me and helped me so much — fellows like Frank Shellenback, Donie Bush, Joe Cronin, and Joe McCarthy. I am thinking of Eddie Collins, who had so much faith in me — and to be in the Hall of Fame with him particularly, as well as these other great players, is a great honor. I'm sorry Eddie isn't here today.

I'm thinking too of Tom Yawkey. I have always said it: Tom Yawkey is the greatest owner in baseball. I was lucky to have played on the club he owned and I'm grateful to him for being here today.

But I'd not be leveling if I left it at that. Ball players are not born great. They're not born great hitters or pitchers or managers, and luck isn't the big factor. No one has come up with a substitute for hard work. I've never met a great player who didn't have to work harder at learning to play ball than anything else he ever did. To me it was the greatest fun I ever had, which probably explains why today I feel both humility and pride, because God let me play the game and I learned to be good at it.

The other day Willie Mays hit his 522nd home run. He has gone past me, and he's pushing and I say to him, "Go get 'em Willie." Baseball gives every American boy a chance to excel. Not just to be as good as someone else, but to be better. This is the nature of man and the name of the game. I hope that some day Satchel Paige and Josh Gibson will be voted into the Hall of Fame as symbols of the great Negro Players who are not here only because they weren't given the chance. As time goes on I'll be thinking baseball, teaching baseball and arguing for baseball to keep it right on top of American sports, just as it is in Japan, Mexico, Venezuela and other Latin and South American countries. I know Casey Stengel feels the same way. . . . I also know I'll lose a dear friend if I don't stop talking. I'm eating into his time, and that is unforgivable. So in closing, I am grateful and know how lucky I was to have been born an American and had a chance to play the game I loved, the greatest game.

Acknowledgments

I wouldn't have gotten to first base on this project without help from a number of people. First among them was Louise Kaufman, who helped me get into the ballpark.

Thanks also to Linda Cann, Floyd Preston, John Henry Williams, Rich Eschen, Hank Aaron, Stan Musial, Pat Kelly (Hall of Fame Library), Glenna Prime, Bill and Karen Wilder, Don Bastian, Angel Guerra, Kevin Linder, and Brian O'Donnell.

And of course, thank you to Ted Williams, who, thank God, views persistence as a virtue.

— JIM PRIME